A Modern Guide to the Book of Genesis

The First Dysfunctional Family

14646

The First Dysfunctional Family

A Modern Guide to the
Book of Genesis

CREST BOOKS

The Salvation Army National Publications
Alexandria, Virginia

Published by Crest Books, Salvation Army National Headquarters
615 Slaters Lane, Alexandria, Virginia 22314
(703) 299–5558 Fax: (703) 684–5539
http://www.salvationarmyusa.org

Printed in the United States of America

Composition by Jennifer Williams
Cover design by Laura Ezzell

Library of Congress Control Number: 2004106407

ISBN: 0-9740940-2-1

To my parents, Ray and Betty Wilson

For much of my life I have been greeted by "Oh, you're Ray and Betty's boy." Maybe now I have lived long enough or accomplished enough to have my folks occasionally greeted with "Oh, you're Ken's parents."

Thanks for your love and encouragement, modeling holiness and Christlikeness in everything—and for teaching me how to write a complete sentence! Being part of this family has been an adventure in itself.

Lord, You have assigned me my portion and my cup;
You have made my lot secure. The boundary lines have fallen
for me in pleasant places; surely I have a delightful inheritance.

—*Psalm 16:5–6*

Contents

Foreword

One of the joys of serving as a training principal is to observe the growth and development of former cadets. This has certainly been the case in my association with Ken Wilson. Ken has always had a longing to relate the timeless, eternal truths of the word of God to our contemporary, changing world. He has indeed accomplished this in the pages of *The First Dysfunctional Family*.

Writing with deep insight into human nature, Ken reminds us that the more things change, the more they remain the same—"There is nothing new under the sun" (Ecclesiastes 1:9). Reading this work is like reading the latest edition of the newspaper. The author tells it like it is with no holds barred. Yet the book is more than just a record of the failures of the families in Genesis. It is matched in content by what life could be by the grace of God. With this book, we can learn from the mistakes of those who have preceded us, and then get on with becoming the people God intended us to be.

Often spiced with humor, *The First Dysfunctional Family* explains not only what is recorded in the Genesis account but also what is left out. Reading it will prove to be a stimulating experience, I can assure you. The author, possessing the rare gift of "sanctified imagination," encourages us to ponder the actions of our ancestors and to thank God for His never–failing, enabling grace.

The First Dysfunctional Family is a book you will not soon forget.

General Bramwell H. Tillsley (Rtd)

Introduction

Where Did We Go Wrong?

Ye sinners lost of Adam's race
Partakers of the fall;
Come and be saved by Jesus' grace,
And crown Him Lord of all.

—*Edward Perronet*

We don't need a seminary education to comprehend some basic things about the Bible. What we do need is to realize that most of the characters who fill its pages are no different from ourselves. If we see them simply as real people—not as grandiose theological concepts or abstract sermon illustrations—then our perception of their behaviors and intentions, their motives and values may become clearer.

Like them, we are all members of families and extended families. We have a wide variety of experience in observing and participating in complex relationships, and we can rely on this experience to interpret the Bible from a common ground. Since most of Scripture deals with family relationships—God our Father, Christ our Brother, adoption, inheritance—we, as readers, become more than just a community of believers. We begin to see families in the Bible as our own families— tackling and resolving problems with spouses and children while confronting the human dilemmas of old age, dishonesty, rebellion, and disobedience. Although the environment may be removed from our particular frame of reference, Bible families are just like ours—as loving and caring and, at times, as violently out of control and dysfunctional.

And perhaps the most dysfunctional family of all was the first one—our first parents, Adam and Eve.

All characters in the Book of Genesis were premodern. Author Gene E. Veith, Jr., states in his book *Postmodern Times: A Christian Guide to Contemporary Thought and Culture* that "premodern people believed in the supernatural. . . . The culture as a whole believed in God (or gods). Life in that world owed its existence and meaning to a spiritual realm beyond the senses." Adam and Eve knew the personality of God as they walked and talked with Him in the Garden. Yet even though they had direct contact with God, the first family of humankind was as messed up as we are.

Human capacity for dysfunctionality has not decreased over time, however, as we continue to make things difficult by making unfair comparisons, exhibiting conditional love, blaming and shaming, being cold and unfeeling, exhibiting legalism, perfectionism, compulsive and/or addictive behavior and denial. Sin—repeated, studied, and mastered—continues to make the world a dangerous place. So, where did our ancestors go wrong? Where did we?

The Bible's themes and the families who are interwoven in them portray patterns of creation, loss, education, redemption, and completion:

> **Creation**—God makes everything in a state of innocence and purity in perfect harmony with Him in the Garden of Eden.
>
> **Loss**—Adam and Eve break that relationship of harmony by succumbing to temptation, rebellion, and sin, thus bringing death and suffering into a perfect world.
>
> **Education**—Descendants of Adam and Eve learn to live in obedience to a holy God without being consumed by His perfect holiness.
>
> **Redemption**—God makes His first promise to send the Messiah to restore the relationship severed by sin so that the guilty are brought back into fellowship with Him.
>
> **Completion**—Evil is punished and righteousness is rewarded as God's perfect creation is restored.

Yet, through all the inner conflicts and corresponding cycles of rebellion and reconciliation, God allows these patterns to continue despite how badly we have treated Him—and each other.

According to Chuck Swindoll, author of *The Strong Family*, all parents have several roles essential to the care and development of children and the building of the family unit: identity, responsibility, authority, and conformity. Likewise, kids of every era—from the dysfunctional Genesis family to the present—have had to deal with the same issues. In our own family relationships we strive toward a balance between desiring to do the right thing for all those concerned and wanting our own way.

If we start to view ourselves in relation to the Bible not just as a body of believers but as family, then we must also come to the sobering conclusion that we are stuck with these Bible characters as role models. After all, we can choose our friends and associates but not our relatives. Therefore, what issues do we need to address for us to achieve some degree of balance or sanity within our own families? Let's take a look and trace the generations in the Book of Genesis in an attempt to avoid their mistakes. We may be dysfunctional, but the good news is we don't have to stay that way.

Chapter 1

Adam and Eve

Had It All . . . Lost It All

Not much has changed since the earliest days of Creation. Families are still in turmoil, yet many also manage to thrive and lead meaningful, fulfilling, happy lives. But what makes one family produce a Mother Teresa while another a Charles Manson? Why does one child turn out so well while the other turns out so badly? To discover certain repeated patterns of dysfunctionality, we rely on Scripture, the revelation of the Holy Spirit, and plenty of imagination.

It's All Fun and Games Until . . .

Genesis 1:2 says that the world at one time was formless and empty. (I cannot imagine anything so dismal and unlike God.) But all that changes as God—pre-existent, without beginning or ending, without needs, without rivals, with no insecurities, no fears, and no doubts, who is by nature perfect love—creates someone to shower that love upon: humankind. We read that God created man "in His image"—not that we would look like God, but that we would have the capacity to worship, to give and accept affection, to exhibit goodness, kindness, and love. I know from studying Scripture and attending church that God loves me. That is His nature. What fuels my imagination, though, is that God likes me. With all my faults and weaknesses He actually likes spending time with me, advising me in my decision making, celebrating my victories, comforting me in my defeats, calming my fears, soothing my pain. He wants to be there, the invited guest of honor at the unfolding of my life. God likes you and me so much that He provides for our relationship with Him. He feels the same about all who have accepted His Lordship for their lives, yet there is room for more.

After God created all the animals and such, He told them to "be fruitful and increase in number" (1:22). During that time, males discovered females, females discovered males, and romance began as the genders reveled in the rich desirability of companionship and procreation (see 1:27). Adam and Eve were personally created by God. All the rest came into being when He spoke them into existence. "The Lord God formed the man from the dust of the ground and breathed into his nostrils the breath of life, and the man became a living being" (2:7).

God then took a section of gloriously created real estate and placed the newly made man where he would be safe and happy. In the middle of the Garden, among all the other trees, were the Tree of Life and the Tree of the Knowledge of Good and Evil. Adam could eat anything he liked, but the Lord commanded, "You must not eat from the tree of the knowledge of good and evil, for when you eat of it you will surely die" (2:8,16–17). Was this a test? Was this God's plan to see how quickly the new human could learn or be trusted and obedient? Was Adam's reaction akin to our observing a sign on a park bench that says, "Wet Paint." Once those two special trees made the banned list, they must have become extremely attractive.

How long was Adam alone? It might have been centuries or even millennia, since God's sense of the passing of time is far different from ours. An apt analogy of varying perceptions of time can be found in your own home on Christmas morning. To a sleepy father who cannot bear one more nagging question from his six–year–old child, asking if it is time to open the gifts, "in a minute" is a significant span of time— long enough perhaps to catch a few more moments of rest. To the child, however, "in a minute" is sixty seconds—and not one tick more.

When Moses wrote the book of Genesis years later, he did not include data as to how long Adam was alone in the Garden, or how long Adam and Eve shared their idyllic honeymoon location before things fell apart. But we can imagine that despite having all manner of animal buddies, Adam was probably feeling pretty isolated. So the Lord said,

"It is not good for the man to be alone. I will make a helper suitable for him" (2:18). This is another of God's most creative works, for as we know from the Genesis account, God caused Adam to fall into a deep sleep, much like that dreamless void you experience under anesthesia. During that first recorded surgical procedure, the Lord removed one of Adam's ribs and used it to fashion a suitable companion.

The Lord had promised Adam someone special to love, who would be a helper and companion; a special someone who was the same, but a little bit different. What went through Adam's mind when the Lord woke him and said, "Well, Adam. What do you think?"

When Adam regained his composure, he could hardly find the words. "She's perfect!"

Since the rib was taken from Adam's side, significance has been placed in the belief that God's plan was for Adam and Eve to live as equals. Side–by–side in an intimate relationship, the two would exist together, more complete than either one would apart. In Genesis 2:24, Moses gives the first reference to marriage, that special relationship second only in intimacy and affection to that of God: "For this reason a man will leave his father and mother and be united to his wife, and they will become one flesh." The point we sometimes miss, though, is that "the man and his wife were both naked, and they felt no shame" (2:25). There was no shame, for there was nothing to be ashamed of.

Therefore, if God blessed all the other animals and living things of His creation and instructed them to reproduce their own kind, isn't it unreasonable to expect God to demand celibacy for a married couple? Adam and Eve were created to be together—to share intimacy, affection, and mutual experiences—to bond together and with God. He made them innocent and in love with the command to "be fruitful and increase in number" (1:28), indicating from the start the significance of family. Did they have kids? Yes. We know the first two were sons, Cain and Abel. Were they born in the Garden of Eden—or later?

Another interesting observation is that Genesis 1:28 says that God blessed *them*—referring to both Adam and Eve—to be fruitful and increase in number. The record of God creating man, however, does not appear until Genesis 2:7. Moses, never claiming to have written everything in strict A–B–C format, may have used a flashback technique to inform us in detail of what the Lord had already done in chapter 1. If so, the chapters in Genesis may not be in strict chronological order. Keep this in mind as we explore the remainder of the creation of the world's first—and perhaps most dysfunctional—family.

Looming Disaster

Imagine having the opportunity to walk and talk with God, seeing Him and hearing His voice! That certainly would make prayer much easier. But even as the two lovers spent their days with each other and with God, sin prowled within their paradise. Unfortunately, things took a turn—not for the worse, but for the catastrophic.

One day when Eve was alone, the serpent said to her, "Did God really say, 'You must not eat from any tree in the Garden?'" (3:1). The attack came with a subtlety worthy of the slickest salesman you can imagine. The serpent created doubt by questioning God's instructions and motives. After more small talk, Eve voluntarily said, "We may eat fruit from the trees in the Garden, but God did say, 'You must not eat from the fruit that is in the middle of the Garden, and you must not touch it, or you will die" (3:2). Eve knew there was something sinister about fooling around with that tree since she added, "you must not touch it." That part was not in God's original instruction. But as soon as she added that detail, the tree suddenly became "Wet Paint" appealing.

"No, that's not what happens," the serpent hissed. "You won't die. God just doesn't want you to see things as they really are. He wants to keep you down because if you eat from that tree you'll be just as He is, able to know both good and evil." To Adam and Eve, evil must have been incomprehensible since they had known only innocence and God's tender provision. They had no idea anyone would try to harm them or subvert the truth, for lies and deception were completely foreign to them. Death, too, was an abstract concept since all the pair had ever witnessed was God's creative genius at work.

Thinking that God and Adam would be pleased with her initiative, Eve ate some of the fruit (3:6). "Hey Adam," she shouted to her husband, "this stuff is great. Try it." And as Scripture records, Adam ate—willingly, without the slightest hesitation. It was the first recorded case of "it seemed like a good idea at the time."

Immediately their eyes were opened and they were bombarded by more information than they were prepared to handle. They knew they had done wrong and felt shame for the first time. They looked at each other and themselves and realized they were naked. Feeling embarrassed, Adam and Eve tried to sew fig leaves together to cover themselves—definitely not high fashion. Where there was once purity, there was now the foul-tasting awareness of sin and disobedience—a high price to pay for an education.

Mission accomplished, the serpent had taken off, leaving the pair alone to deal with the consequences of breaking God's prime directive. Satan's mission is still the death of man and the ruin of all of God's best. Anything God loves, Satan hates and wants destroyed. When sin was turned loose on the world, it was like trying to get toothpaste back into the tube. Once done, it could not be undone.

Crime and Punishment

Soon after the incident, Adam and Eve heard God walking in the Garden as was His custom. He looked and called, but no Adam and Eve. We should not assume for a moment that God didn't know what was going on. He planned to confront them so they would understand the consequences of their actions.

"Hey kids, where are you?" God may have called.

Adam answered, "I heard You in the Garden, and I was afraid because I was naked; so I hid" (3:10).

God responded, "Who told you that you were naked? Have you eaten from the tree that I commanded you not to eat from?" (3:11).

Learning the art of spin and denial in a flash, Adam said it was "the woman You put here with me—she gave me some fruit" (3:12).

"Sure Adam, she threatened you and forced you to eat against your will, right?" Adam never admitted to doing anything wrong. Instead, he shifted the responsibility to Eve for giving him the forbidden fruit, and to God for giving him the woman in the first place.

So the Lord asked Eve, "What is this you have done?" to which she replied, "The serpent deceived me, and I ate" (3:13). At last the truth was out—she had been deceived by the serpent. She knew where the misinformation had come from, and it was not from the Lord. But although Eve had been lied to, she still needed to face the responsibility for her disobedience.

Sin cannot be hidden for very long. That is a valuable lesson for all of us, for even though the hammer of judgment does not fall immediately, we should never think that we had gotten away with it. In Psalm 7:14, David explains this by likening sin to a pregnancy: "He who is pregnant with evil and conceives trouble, gives birth to disillusionment." In the early stages of pregnancy there is little visible evidence of what is happening. But soon, you can't miss it. Being "pregnant with evil" is similar. One cruel response, one uncaring act hardly shows. But when sin runs its full course, it gives birth to full–grown rebellion against God. "There is a way that seems right to a man, but in the end it leads to death" (Proverbs 14:12).

The Lord could have looked the other way and just given Adam and Eve a second chance. Had he done that though, God could not be God, for if He is loving, He must be just. If He rewards righteousness, He must also punish sin and rebellion. So the Lord said to the serpent, "Because you have done this, cursed are you above all the livestock and all the wild animals! You will crawl on your belly and you will eat dust all the days of your life. And I will put enmity between you and the woman, and between your offspring and hers; he will crush your head, and you will strike his heel" (Genesis 3:14–15). The serpent will be a snake, crawling on the hot ground, hating and being hated.

The prophecy of enmity between the woman and her offspring may be the first messianic prophecy of Jesus Christ. Satan would bruise His heel—a serious but not eternally fatal injury often equated with Jesus being put to death on the cross. But Jesus would rise from the dead and come again as Risen Lord and Righteous King to crush Satan and the influence of sin forever.

To Eve, God said, "I will greatly increase your pains in childbearing; with pain you will give birth to children. Your desire will be for your husband, and he will rule over you" (3:16). Note that He said "increase your pains in childbearing." That item will be important when we discuss Adam and Eve's kids. As if that was not enough punishment, she would be fated to look to her husband for communication and intimacy, and he, no doubt, would learn to turn a deaf ear to her pleas for meaningful conversation and emotional comfort long before the invention of football, television, and ESPN.

To Adam, God said, "Because you listened to your wife and ate from the tree about which I commanded you . . . cursed is the ground because of you; through painful toil you will eat of it all the days of your life. It will produce thorns and thistles for you, and you will eat the plants of the field. By the sweat of your brow you will eat your food until you return to the ground, since from it you were taken; for dust you are and to dust you will return" (3:17–19). So if you hate your job and dread the thought of going there each day, blame Adam.

Now they would be exposed to the searing heat of the sun, the aches and pains of toil, and the promise that one day, the man who was created for life would die and return to the earth from which he was made. The Lord's promise that humankind would die was not a sudden, drop–dead type of thing, but rather a slow erosion of youth and vigor, sapped by the demands of life. It was a tedious sentence of death, filled with anxiety and heartbreak.

Adam and Eve had lost their innocence and had placed themselves squarely in the path of God's stern correction. What more would the Lord do with the couple now that they had experienced evil along with good? He couldn't leave them in the Garden in their sinful state. God said, "The man has now become like one of Us, knowing good and evil. He must not be allowed to reach out his hand and take also from the Tree of Life and eat, and live forever" (3:22). To keep them from getting into more trouble, the Lord banished Adam and Eve from the Garden. An angel with a flaming sword was positioned by the exit to bar any possible return (see 3:23–24).

Before you think that God was unfair to give them the boot for only one mistake, remember that it was not a mistake or an error in judgment. It was defiant disobedience. And for bringing sin into the world, the punishment had to be severe and decisive. Besides, God's greatest fear was that they would eat from the Tree of Life and live forever in their defiled state without hope of the rest that comes with death. Can you imagine what would have happened had they eaten that fruit? They would still be here—two wrinkled, bitter, spiteful, nasty old people looking like a pair of pitted prunes, choking on their sin and regret.

How long were Adam and Eve in Eden before they ruined it? Probably not very long, given our ability to get into trouble faster than a little boy dressed for church on Easter Sunday can get dirty. If God began creation bright and early Monday morning, finished Saturday and took Sunday off as a day of rest, Adam and Eve may have been on their way out of paradise the following Monday by lunch time! I wish the Bible gave more specific details, for Moses offered only the bare facts for the theology of sin and redemption. What was the total effect of sin on their lives and families?

The Effect of Sin

Lecturing at the Salvation Army International Millennial Congress in 2000, Dr. Robert Tuttle, professor at Asbury Theological Seminary, suggested that Adam and Eve lost the ability to perceive the spiritual dimension with their senses. For two people who had seen God face–to–face, the loss of such a wondrous ability had to have been devastating. We exist in the dimensions of height, width, breadth, motion, and time. All of what we learn comes to us through these dimensions, based on sensory data, intuition, or past experience. We cannot see God, however, and survive because of sin's corrupting influence. Even Moses was only allowed to "see" God in the form of a burning bush or to catch a glimpse of the back of God's goodness as He passed by. Now Adam and Eve had also become "outsiders."

The two knew they had done wrong, but there was nothing they could say or do to make it right. They had lost the capacity to find the way back to where they had been in their relationship with God. But they also lost intimacy with each other. Once Adam and Eve had no secrets. God shared with them everything they needed to grow and become "one flesh."

Perhaps the Lord had planned to withhold the fruit of the Tree of the Knowledge of Good and Evil until the day Adam and Eve might have been able to handle it as a gift from their heavenly Father. Instead, they would grope for answers without ever being completely sure of the outcome. They had been sentenced to the next phase of their young lives—to raise a family, earn a living, survive in the outside world without direct, personal contact with their Creator. At no point in history have two people been so woefully ill–prepared as parents—of the entire human race.

My theory is when Adam and Eve were banished from Eden, they fled in such a hurry that they left behind information they would surely need later. On the dining room table they left several instruction manuals—*The Complete Guide to Understanding Women for Men, The Complete Guide to Understanding Men for Women,* and *The Complete Guide to Raising Children.* Without this essential data, we have been flying by the collective seats of our pants, trying to figure things out ever since.

Chapter 2

The Next Generation

Murder and Madness

I would not have wanted to live in Adam and Eve's household after their expulsion from Eden. Where once there had been intimacy and fun, now there was bitterness, blame, and constant argument. They had been driven out into the world to fend for themselves, receiving less direct care and nurture from God. Their children certainly would have added a new dimension to their forced voyage of discovery, as well. Adam and Eve had no parents or grandparents to turn to for advice; no one to explain what to do for diaper rash, or how to make a diaper in the first place; no one to tell them the difference between a sniffle and something more serious. After the Fall, they were orphans without the constant guiding presence of God. We at least have the assurance of Jesus' promise that "I will not leave you comfortless—as orphans in the world. I will come to you" (John 14:18). Adam and Eve had none of that.

In or Out?

Children bless us beyond measure and complicate our lives beyond belief. We know that Adam and Eve's first set of children were Cain and his younger brother Abel. Their names are recorded in Genesis 4:1–2: "Adam lay with his wife Eve, and she became pregnant and gave birth to Cain. She said, 'With the help of the Lord I have brought forth a man.' Later she gave birth to his brother Abel. Now Abel kept flocks, and Cain worked the soil." From one reference we know the parents, how the children were conceived, their birth order, and occupations.

A key question arises here: How much time is left unaccounted for and unrecorded between Genesis 1:27–28, where God created man, both male and female, and told them to "increase in number," and 4:1–2, where the conception and birth of Cain and Abel is described? Returning to the question, *Were Cain and Abel born in the Garden of Eden or after the Fall,* the popular response is "after," citing the Scripture references concerning conception and childbirth in the order of the chapters in Moses' account. But what if Moses, like any good storyteller, took some information out of chronological sequence?

As stated earlier, God created Adam and Eve to be "one flesh," allowing a special intimacy that comes in a pure love relationship between a husband and wife. If God expected and permitted as much from the plants and animals, isn't it reasonable that He had the same expectation for the couple He fashioned with His own hands? If God made man to lavish His infinite affection on, might He not also extend a similar opportunity for mankind to respond with love to create their own offspring?

Further evidence leading to the conclusion that Adam and Eve had children before the Fall is found in that first reference to Cain: "Adam lay with his wife Eve, and she became pregnant and gave birth to Cain. She said, 'With the help of the Lord I have brought forth a man'" (4:1). The key phrase is "with the help of the Lord," indicating His loving kindness and interest in humankind in spite of how shabbily they had responded to His generosity.

An additional detail supports the theory that Cain and Abel were born in Eden. It is found in Moses' later reference to their brother Seth. Moses chronicles the growth of the extended family through multiple generations: "This is the written account of Adam's line. When God created man, He made him in the likeness of God. He created them male and female and blessed them. . . . When Adam had lived 130 years, he had a son in his own likeness, in his own image; and he named him Seth" (5:1–3). The key phrase here is "in his own likeness, in his own image." Adam and Eve were created "in the image of God." To state that Seth, on the other hand, was born resembling his earthly father might suggest that the first two children may have shared with their parents in the unique creation relationship with God back in Eden. (It is also interesting to note that Adam's age was given in this accounting, a frame of reference not used in the Bible until people began to die.)

A citation often used to argue the birth of Cain and Abel as having occurred after the Fall is the Lord's judgment on Eve: "I will greatly increase your pains in childbearing; with pain you will give birth to children" (3:16). This statement could be interpreted as a reference to an act that has not yet occurred. Yet the intriguing aspect of this edict is the phrase "greatly *increase* your pains in childbearing." What if prior births had not presented any more discomfort than a mild headache or leg cramp? Imagine Eve waiting through nine months of pregnancy without mood swings, hormonal changes, or morning sickness. And then one evening as the two were naming some of the animals, suppose Eve nudged Adam and said, "Honey, it's time." With a painless push or two, they may have found themselves with a miniature person. That would be an ideal every parent would dearly love to experience! It all centers on the interpretation of that word *increase*. Why mention an increase if nothing had occurred to make the comparison?

If the Heart Is Not Right

If Cain and Abel were born inside the Garden and experienced all that Eden had to offer, did they feel its loss as keenly as their parents? Did they suffer the shame and disappointment of being banished and carry the weighty responsibility for the family's misery upon their own shoulders? Before the Fall they were siblings without rivalry. Then they joined their parents in the newly formed ranks of the dysfunctional, blaming and being blamed for their problems.

Here is an idea to consider. The Bible records Cain and Abel—but were there girls? With few exceptions (Ruth, Rahab, and a few others) writers of the Bible rarely accounted for the females. If childbirth did not hurt, could Adam and Eve have had a small army of girls before, during, and after they had Cain and Abel? That would have certainly fulfilled the fruitful and multiply command. An angel might well be needed for crowd control to keep that mob from returning to the Garden.

I feel sorry for Adam and his messed–up brood. Imagine the unrelenting tension each night at the dinner table—Mom and Dad fighting over who was tempted first or whose fault it was that they were stuck outside of Eden. Every night, years lengthening into centuries, sin's poison was working its way into memories and beliefs. If what you believe influences what you do, and what you do determines who you become, then they must have become more and more miserable.

We know very little of Cain and Abel except their occupations and their later lives. Cain the farmer worked the cursed ground, desperate to produce enough food to keep the family alive. Being the first parental experiment, the prototype, Cain must have felt that he should have had a chance to stay in Eden. After all, it was Mom and Dad who ruined everything, not him.

Was Abel the cooperative son, the one to whom Cain was compared, the one Cain deeply resented? Did Abel remember Eden and long to keep part of the memory alive without falling prey to the sin all around him? Was he just glad to have the opportunity to live and have some relationship with God—no matter how remote or fragile?

Did the parents of this noncompliant firstborn have to deal with the screaming tantrums and compare his behavior to their angelic second child? If Abel exhibited all the enthusiasm and charm, but never the stubborn streak of his sibling, would an unfavorable comparison have been made, so common in dysfunctional families, which often causes one child to feel superior and the other to feel like an outcast?

As the brothers grew, Cain brought some of his vegetables as an offering to the Lord. But Abel brought choice cuts of meat from some of his flock. The Lord was pleased with Abel and his offering, but not with Cain and his. Why was Abel's offering accepted and not Cain's? Some have postulated that Abel's was accepted because it was a blood offering of the sinless for the guilty, as a precursory object lesson in anticipation of Christ's atoning death on the cross. Cain offered vegetables—big deal. No life was taken; no innocent for the guilty.

Hebrews 11:4 states that Abel's sacrifice was superior because it was an offering of a life and that it was offered in faith. The aspect of a faith offering is correct because Abel trusted and loved God to the extent that only his best would be suitable. But God had not yet set any standard for an acceptable offering. That would come much later, as Moses wrote down the law with all of its rules and regulations designed to teach the nation of Israel to worship in holiness and truth.

It is hard to imagine God looking with disdain on anyone's best offering of who they are and what they do. He would not hold a shepherd in higher regard than a farmer, or a corporate executive as more significant than an auto mechanic. God simply expects the best of who we are. He expects a willing heart and a positive attitude, genuine regret for sin and equally genuine desire for forgiveness, and a spirit thankful for His provision and care. God did not berate Cain for the vegetables; the offering was not accepted because Cain's heart was not right. If the heart is right, then the motives are right, the worship is right, and the offering is accepted. Break that chain and the offering is just another bushel of spuds.

God would have gladly helped Cain had he asked, but Cain's bitterness would not allow him to show weakness. Then the Lord said to Cain, "Why are you angry? Why is your face downcast? If you do what is right, will you not be accepted? But if you do not do what is right, sin is crouching at your door; it desires to have you, but you must master it" (4:3–7). God wanted Cain to deal with his attitude problems before it was too late.

God referred to that sin of bitterness as being like a predator "crouching at your door." Stated another way: "Be self–controlled and alert. Your enemy the devil prowls around like a roaring lion looking for someone to devour. Resist him, standing firm in the faith" (1 Peter 5:8–9). Put simply, deal with the sin before it eats you alive.

Out from the Lord's Presence

Scripture offers no buildup to the story. Cain simply says to Abel, "Let's go out to the field" (Genesis 4:8). Rather than explaining Cain's actions away as a crime of passion, the Bible makes it clear that this is premeditated murder. Cain lured Abel out into the fields, away from any witnesses, with the single intent of ridding himself of his hated little brother. The Bible does not specify the type of injury or the weapon used, but it was most likely a rock or club to the head. If Genesis 4:11 is to be taken literally, then a blunt–force trauma would certainly create massive loss of "your brother's blood from your hand." Where did Cain get the idea that he could kill his brother if he hit him hard enough, since no one had died yet? While animals had been killed, there had been no precedent for human death.

The Lord asked Cain, "Where is your brother, Abel?"—a question much like those parents ask, not for information but to elicit a response. God had used the same interrogation method when He asked Adam and Eve about the forbidden fruit. Cain's unemotional reaction to God is amazing. Was he thinking, *Am I supposed to account for the little brat all the time? He got what he deserved because he ticked me off* (see 4:9–10). Cain responded with an icy, "I don't know. Am I my brother's keeper?" But he knew where Abel was and what had happened to him.

"What have you done?" the Lord asked. He already knew what had happened but needed to see if Cain fully appreciated the effect of his actions. "Your brother's blood cries out to Me from the ground" (4:10). "I know what you did," the Lord continued. "Don't think you got away with it. You will be driven from this land, for it reeks of your brother's freshly–spilled blood. You will work the land but it will not grow crops for you, no matter what you do. You will have no place to call your own and will be 'a restless wanderer on the earth'" (4:12).

Cain had not been remorseful at first, but then he broke down when confronted with his punishment. He did not care that Abel was dead, or that God was angry, or that his parents would grieve the loss of their son. But the thought of his own mortality terrified him: "Whoever finds me will kill me" (4:14).

We do not know the age of Cain or Abel at the time of the murder, but we do know that Cain had the emotional maturity of a teenager who had not yet made the connection between actions and consequences. Teens can go from being agreeable and cooperative to disrespectful and foul–mouthed in a flash, driving their parents crazy in the process. And just as quickly, they revert back, not understanding why their parents are so upset. It was as if Cain had said, "So I made a mistake and I'm sorry you feel bad, God. But that was then and this is now." As in some teenage apologies today—demonstrating no repentance, admitting no wrong, owning up to no consequences—the responsibility is diverted: "I'm sorry you feel that way."

Murder is a big deal to God, not something that can be allowed to just fade away. It is not a case of "we have thought about that long enough, it is time to move on." Cain had to take his punishment, yet in a characteristic display of unmerited kindness, the Lord marked Cain in some manner with the warning that anyone who harmed him would be killed himself, and their families would suffer revenge seven times over. Was the mark a tattoo? A change in physical appearance? Perhaps the Lord allowed Cain to live with some manifestation of his guilt. Maybe Cain was the first one to be seen walking around town pushing a shopping cart and muttering to himself about aliens and conspiracies. Whatever it was, it was as easy to spot as a person wearing a bright orange Department of Corrections prison uniform.

In Revelation 7:1–8 the Lord gives marks of protection to 144,000 faithful witnesses during the perilous last days of mankind. They will be identified so as not to be harmed in any way as they make one last attempt to communicate the gospel to a world on the verge of a violent end. But isn't that just like God to have compassion even as the entire universe He created is being rolled up like a pull–down window shade?

The next comment about Cain is perhaps one of the saddest in the Bible. "So Cain went out from the Lord's presence and lived in the land of Nod, east of Eden" (4:16). He went from the Lord's presence—how far can that be? Is there anywhere that God is not? The universe and everything in it is His—including Nod. Centuries later, King David would learn this same fate the hard way after he conspires to kill his trusted friend Uriah following an adulterous affair with Uriah's wife.

> Where can I go from Your Spirit? Where can I flee from Your presence? If I go up to the heavens, You are there; if I make my bed in the depths, You are there. If I rise on the wings of the dawn, if I settle on the far side of the sea, even there Your hand will guide me, Your right hand will hold me fast (Psalm 139:7–10).

From Two Flawed Sons

The Bible recorded the births of Cain and Abel, but were there daughters within this sad family unit? Writers of the Bible rarely accounted for females, with the exceptions of Ruth, Rahab, and a few others. Could daughters have been born to Adam and Eve, daughters whose lives simply went unrecorded? The next child we know of was Seth, who was made "in the likeness of Adam" and clearly born in the post–Eden era—never having experienced any of its blessings. "Adam lay with his wife again, and she gave birth to a son and named him Seth, saying, 'God has granted me another child in place of Abel, since Cain killed him" (Genesis 4:25). Nothing much was written about Seth, good or bad, despite his unenviable role as the replacement child. What a burden that must have been! Eve must have watched him like a hawk and protected him from the slightest danger. In due course, Seth had a son and named him Enoch.

Surmounting his tendencies for nomadic wanderings and his lack of a relationship with God, Cain founded great cities. He also had children, and although one of his sons was likewise named Enoch, the two family lines followed radically divergent paths. Cain's grandsons raised huge herds of livestock, composed wonderful works of music, and fashioned artistic creations in copper and bronze. Cain's legacy, however, filled as it was with enterprising tenacity and creative energy, was most noted for its intense hatred of family. Cain's anger carried over multiple generations until that dysfunction became part of his family's heritage.

With one son dead and the other banished, Adam and Eve certainly had tasted the fruit and knew good and evil, yet they had not acquired the spiritual backbone to know how to control it. They had unleashed evil into the world, their first victims being those closest to them. Such is usually the case when we sin. We may think sin harms no one but ourselves. In reality, it first affects our children, who see and imitate our behaviors. The act of children killing children began with two flawed sons, who bore the brunt of the sin from their equally flawed parents.

Although the birth process involves more pain, it thankfully continues. Humans have not yet stopped the perpetuation of our kind, both good and bad. The pain of childbirth, after all, is forgotten over time. What is not so easily forgotten by a parent is the agony of a child's unfulfilled potential. That kind of painful disappointment lingers as we watch our children grow into killers, abusers, and criminals—all squandering the possibilities of life.

We all come into the world in basically the same way. In fact, with the exception of Adam and Eve, every child since Cain came connected to their mother by an umbilical cord. As such, we all bear the mark of membership in the human race—regardless of gender, ethnicity, race, or religion. The Lord may forgive, guide, and often guard us from ourselves, but He does not remove the responsibility and accountability we have for our actions or for the influence we have on others, including our children—even if they live to be hundreds of years of age.

Chapter 3

Among a Bunch of Geezers

One Who Found the Way

When I was a kid, I thought my parents and grandparents seemed old. From my perspective, they were. They dressed much more formally than I did—or do now. In fact, I cannot recall my father ever wearing jeans and a sweatshirt. But now that I am their age, I don't feel old, and neither did they. It was just my perception that was skewed.

Scripture notes that the "average" length of human life was about seventy years—a poetic "three score and ten"—or maybe eighty if we had the strength (see Psalm 90:10). Thanks to modern medicine we have increased that average slightly. Are we happier and more fulfilled? Do we feel "accomplished" with the time we have been allotted? As the Bible reveals, "length of stay" is not the only goal.

Genesis lists the all-time oldies who make even the most geriatric of our day seem like mere infants. But if their only claim to fame is their duration, then all we really had was a bunch of geezers.

The roster of the "mega-superannuated" begins in chapter 5 with Adam. It states that he lived to be 930 years old and did not father Seth until age 130. Can you imagine Seth in Little League asking his dad to play catch? Adam would have been about 140. In Seth's eyes, how old would someone have been to be considered truly old—800, 900? The list continues with each generation's age at the time their first son and primary heir was born, along with their total life span. With these numbers, an undertaker would have starved to death between jobs!

- Seth was 105 when son Enosh was born, and lived another 807 years with sons and daughters until he finally died at age 912 (5:6–8).

- Enosh, Adam's grandson, had son Kenan at 90. Enosh died young, though, at 815 (5:9–11).

- Kenan, Adam's great grandson, had son Mahalalel at 70. Kenan died at the age of 910 (5:12–14).

- Mahalalel was a virtual child himself at 65 when he had his son Jared. Mahalalel lived another 830 years and died at 895. He would have been Adam's great, great grandson (5:15–17).

- Jared, Adam's great, great, great grandson was 162 when he had Enoch. Jared lived another 800 years, dying at age 932 (5:19–20).

- Enoch, another child–parent, was 65 when he had Methuselah, the geriatric record holder of all time.

Scripture says that Enoch, Adam's great, great, great, great grandson lived another 300 years and that he "walked with God; then he was no more, because God took him away" (5:21–24). There is no death recorded for Enoch—the Lord just took him away to Glory, at age 365. We'll investigate Enoch more at length, since he was the only one of his line that correctly combined longevity with spiritual maturity.

Methuselah became the father of Lamech at age 187, and he died at the overripe old age of 969 (5:25–27). To put his age in perspective—assuming their years to be comparable to ours—if Methuselah had been born at the time of the Norman invasion and the Battle of Hastings in 1066, he still would not be gone until 2035!

When Lamech had lived 182 years he had a son named Noah, who would gain fame as a world–class shipwright and captain of the Ark. Lamech lived to be 777 before he died, and he prayed that Noah "will comfort us in the labor and painful toil of our hands caused by the ground the Lord has cursed" (5:28–31).

When Noah was 500 years old he had three sons named Ham, Shem, and Japheth. But God had other plans for Noah, which surpassed merely joining a roster of old men who lived long but accomplished little—with the exception of Enoch.

Quality vs. Quantity

As a Salvation Army officer and son of officer parents, I continue to meet retired officers who worked with my folks and who have stories about my childhood. Can you imagine those early generations in Genesis and the stories they must have had about the children growing up? They were probably making comments about "that little rascal," who, by then, was well into his 800s.

The band of extreme seniors must have nonchalantly let their lives go by, allowing the centuries to solidify their stubborn ways, because shortly thereafter, the Lord decided to limit the life span to 120 years. Apparently, the opportunity of a long life does not necessary create the desire to accomplish greater things. Unlike fine cheeses and antiques, dysfunctionality and sin never improve with age.

Mozart, who died at the age of thirty–four, accomplished an extraordinary amount of work in his brief life: fifty–six symphonies, fifteen operas, and thousands of other complex musical works according to *Encyclopedia Britannica*. Would he have created much more if given longer to live, or would he have begun to waste those additional centuries of opportunity?

Wouldn't it have been wonderful to live longer—and *not* take for granted all the things that life had to offer? If we had this ability today, I might like to try bungee jumping and hang gliding well into my 700s or 800s, or perhaps I would take more time to write or study, to do whatever my mind and heart could conceive without worrying about being too old. God's lesson, however, is to make every moment count, regardless of how long we have to live.

Among the bunch of biblical geezers there was one who understood this and did something truly remarkable with his life.

Enoch

While on a long drive, my wife was reading the story of Enoch in Genesis when she asked, "How did he know what God expected? Without the law, the patriarchs and prophets, how did he know what was the right thing to do?"

How *did* Enoch know? There was no Scripture until Moses wrote it years later. Without Scripture, there was no law. Without the law, how did people know if they had broken it? If there was no commonly known standard of right or wrong, no accepted code of ethical behavior, how could anyone be held accountable?

Since it would be years before the Ten Commandments codified rules of responsible worship and civil cooperation, perhaps revelation came directly from God speaking to the patriarchs, reminding them of His expectations. But it seems more logical that revelation came from the family. The family shared stories that related actions to consequences, told from parent to child over the span of centuries. All important instruction was passed down this way. Families today still do the same—they share stories at Thanksgiving, Christmas, or any special gathering.

From a time framework, it would have been possible for Enoch to ask his great, great, great, great grandpa Adam, "What was it like in the Garden when you walked with God in the cool of the day?" Enoch's question would not have been intended to berate Adam, but to discover what that deep relationship with God was all about before sin ruined everything. I believe Adam took great delight in answering all of Enoch's questions. Enoch may not have been the only one to understand the magnitude of what was lost, but he was most probably the only one to realize the incredible value of the relationship he still had with God.

"You do not have, because you do not ask God." (James 4:2)

In those early days, Enoch learned from his family. But was family the only thing he had? Did he not also have prayer?

Only a few long–lived generations before Enoch, some time after Seth had his son Enosh (Enoch's great, great grandfather), "men began to call on the name of the Lord" (4:26). The Bible does not indicate whether men called in worship, or if it was a desperate call for help, but Enoch, whose name means "to dedicate or to instruct," sought the Lord's direction and called on Him to help change his heart.

Unwilling to perpetuate the family tradition of blame and shame—the rehashing of the loss of Eden and its effects—Enoch concentrated all of his energy on the Lord. Unlike King Solomon, who asked for wisdom to rule Israel and to know right from wrong (see 1 Kings 3), Enoch did not ask for wisdom. I believe he asked for holiness instead. Having grown up with the stories of the Fall and its aftermath, Enoch knew that he did not have the spiritual discipline to change on his own. He understood that he would not be able to *learn* holiness. Holiness would have to come directly from God.

Enoch instinctively knew what is echoed in Hebrews 12:14: "Make every effort to live in peace with all men and to be holy; without holiness no one will see the Lord." He wanted to know God, see God, hear God, and have fellowship with God, as two friends of like mind and heart might walk along together. The Lord honored Enoch's request for holiness to such a degree that he was able to see God and survive.

Scripture says that Enoch walked with God, side by side in deep conversation. It later states that Enoch did not die, at least as we know or experience it. To a cynic it would appear that he vanished one day and was never found. But wouldn't someone have found his remains or some clue as to his whereabouts? The simplest explanation is that the Lord and Enoch went walking and talking, discussing life, eternity, and creation, until they had gone so far that it was just too late and too far for Enoch to return. God may have suggested that Enoch might as well come home with Him and continue the conversation uninterrupted— "Enoch walked with God; then he was no more, because God took him away" (Genesis 5:24). In the roll call of the heroes of faith, we read:

> By faith Enoch was taken from this life, so that he did not experience death; he could not be found, because God had taken him away. For before he was taken, he was commended as one who pleased God (Hebrews 11:5–6).

What a way to go!

The next verse in Hebrews states the necessity of being like Enoch if we are to please God and experience the Lord's favor: "Without faith it is impossible to please God, because anyone who comes to Him must believe that He exists and that He rewards those who earnestly seek Him." This is wise counsel for all who would break free from typical patterns of family dysfunction.

Lessons Learned

Scripture can be distilled into basic themes—righteousness is rewarded, evil is punished, and all the rest shows how to walk and talk with God. All of Scripture either points us to Him and how to enter that love relationship of grace that was broken in Eden, or it directs our life with Him once we know Him as Lord.

From the story of Enoch we learn two things. First, we need to interact with previous generations, learn from their wisdom and hear their personal accounts of history. We need to hear our grandparents share embarrassing stories of our parents' exploits as children so that we can see our parents as normal people who made some of the same mistakes we made while growing up.

Second, our connection to God is maintained in our communication with Him—through our behaviors and our prayers. Always abundantly patient, God delights in fulfilling the needs of His people. He longs to hear our prayers. "While we are still speaking," He hears us and is sending the answer along (see Isaiah 65:24). Sometimes His answer is yes—God gives us what we have asked for. At other times, however, His answer is no—either what we want is not in His plan, or we are not living according to His will. But we must keep praying until something changes—the request, the circumstance, or us.

Chapter 4

Noah

A Second Chance

Unfortunately for the human race, Enoch's quest for holiness was never duplicated in his children or relatives. In fact, things got much worse as people experimented with sin in all its permutations. Like a malevolent virus, sin poisoned every aspect of life and society—a situation not so different from ours today. In an effort to make sure truth and righteousness would survive, the Lord decided to deal with the pervasive nature of sin with water—lots of water—and the help of a righteous man named Noah.

Although much in Scripture is written about the fallen condition of mankind, there is little describing the actual flood or the interaction of Noah's family—the one saved community of believers. When viewed from a family perspective, the book of Genesis begins with a single community of believers—Adam and Eve. The community grows, as children are born and new generations are added, until ten generations later, the community is again reduced to a family unit. Back to square one, you might say.

An Unruly Mess

Chapter 6 of Genesis introduces the scene by describing what demographers might call a "population growth trend." But as families grew in population, so did their capacity for rebellion.

> When men began to increase in number on the earth and
> daughters were born to them, the sons of God saw that
> the daughters of men were beautiful, and they married
> any of them they chose. Then the Lord said, "My Spirit
> will not contend with man forever, for he is mortal; his
> days will be 120 years." The Nephilim were on the earth
> in those days—and also afterward—when the sons of
> God went to the daughters of men and had children by
> them (6:1–4).

First, let us clarify what defines the Nephilim. Some have thought
that they were pagans like the giant–sized sons of Anak whom Moses'
spies saw on their reconnaissance mission into Canaan (see Numbers
13:26–33). Some think Goliath was one of these Nephilim. All agree that
these people cared nothing for the things of God. They were vicious
"professional sinners," who took what they wanted whenever they
wanted it. God saw that "every inclination of the thoughts of the heart
[of mankind] was only evil all the time" (6:5).

Next, we come face to face with a posed theory concerning who the
"sons of God" might be. Do they represent fallen angelic beings? Were
angels marrying humans back then? Anyone with a rudimentary
knowledge of high school biology can see problems with this idea.
Angels and humans are vastly different; one is immortal, the other, not.
Scripture says that God created man "a little lower than the angels"
(Hebrews 2:7). Close, but not close enough. In the animal world when
two species are interbred, issues arise. For example, when the donkey
and the horse are bred together, the mule is the outcome—a perfectly
acceptable animal with excellent traits from both lines, but sterile.
Mules don't have little mules. The same could be true for angels and
humans. What might be a more logical interpretation?

After Adam and Eve, the lineage followed two major families—the
descendants of Cain and those of Seth. Remember, the family of Cain
had been marked in some way as being contrary to the things of God.
Alternately, the family of Seth were to have aligned themselves with the
things of God. With the exception of Enoch, however, the Sethites were
not much better than their Cainite relatives. Moses may have referred to

Seth's family line as the "sons of God," as much hoping for their redemption as lamenting how far they had fallen.

At first, a clearly defined division of families existed. But soon families too big to be controlled by the dominant father figures of Seth or Cain began to move into new areas to settle. These extended family units branched out to become clans and tribes, intermarrying not just for love but to maintain political alliances and to strengthen their numbers. These increased intermarriages blurred the original family lines with each succeeding generation.

Imagine that the line of Cain is yellow and the line of Seth is blue. Both are distinct primary colors. But when you mix yellow and blue, you get green. With each generation, there were more and more greens and fewer true blues and yellows. By the time of Noah, there were more shades of blue and yellow and green than in a super–deluxe crayon box. If the lines of right and wrong were as unclearly indicated—and the people as indistinguishable from one another, then who could be considered righteous?

God's comment, "My Spirit will not contend with man forever" (Genesis 6:3), indicates just how big a pain mankind had developed into and how weary the Lord had become with the world's sin. God's great love project was broken almost beyond repair. So what was the Lord to do? He was going to erase all that He had so joyfully made in the first place: "I will wipe mankind, whom I have created, from the face of the earth—men and animals, and creatures that move along the ground, and birds of the air—for I am grieved that I have made them" (6:7).

But if God can make it, why can't He just remake it? Recreating everything would be no harder for God than erasing a blackboard and writing on it again. A righteous God, however, must make sure He is fair and just in all things. He has no room for "collateral damage" as He metes out justice and executes judgment for sin while protecting the righteous who might get caught in the crossfire.

Should God's act of destroying everything be construed as a petulant fit of anger? Hardly. Only His abundant patience kept the entire human race from obliteration, since it is the Lord's way to save a righteous remnant from harm. So despite regret of having made man in the first place, God provided for a second chance.

Exclusive Seating

As the Lord looked around, He found Noah, "a righteous man, blameless among the people of his time. . . . God said to Noah, 'I am going to put an end to all people . . . and the earth. So make yourself an ark of cypress wood; make rooms in it and coat it with pitch inside and out'" (6:9,13–14).

We see the word "ark" several times in the Bible, and all refer to containers of deliverance—of the human race and animal kingdom (Noah); of a person—an ark of reeds to deliver Moses from Pharaoh's death decree; and the Ark of the Covenant—a chest made of acacia wood, overlaid with pure gold to save the hearts and souls of a people called to be holy.

The entire vessel was to be 450 feet long, 75 feet wide, and 45 feet high, with three distinct levels or decks. It was to have a finished roof and side bulkheads that came to 18 inches from the top of the superstructure for ventilation and light. It was to have a door in the side rather than on the top deck for ease of entry of cargo, supplies, and passengers (see 6:15–16). Noah must have felt a bit overwhelmed at this point wondering how to construct this monstrous backyard project, but the Scripture record is a concept drawing, not a blueprint. I am sure that the Lord gave Noah more specific instructions as the project developed—mitered corners, mortise and tenon joints, pegs instead of deck screws—to create an engineering marvel, built far from any major body of water. Since the ark was not steerable and had no means of propulsion, it was more like a floating barn than a boat, traveling where the winds and currents carried it. (Perhaps this is the first use of the phrase "going with the flow.") Had Columbus taken an ark on his voyage of discovery, he might still be bobbing along the Atlantic looking for a place to land.

The Lord went on to explain: "I am going to bring floodwaters on the earth to destroy all life under the heavens, every creature that has the breath of life in it. Everything on earth will perish. But I will establish My covenant with you, and you will enter the ark—you and your sons and your wife and your sons' wives with you" (6:17–18). I can well imagine Noah sighing with relief when the Lord interjected the word "but" right after He said everything in the world would perish, finally explaining that Noah's family would be saved. But the Lord was very specific in His guest list for this "second chance cruise." Everyone outside of Noah's immediate family was in line for punishment. Noah would need all his resolve to shut the door and bar it fast once the floods came and drowning friends and neighbors began pounding on the hull.

Noah got right to work building the ark and making all the necessary preparations. The Lord instructed him as to how many of each type of animal to take along with enough food for the animals and human passengers. If animals died on the voyage, Noah had replacements (see 6:19–20; 7: 2,3). He did all that the Lord commanded and completed the work when he was 600 years old—impressive for an old guy. (I also think the Lord managed to strengthen Noah to deal with the ridicule he must have received from the Nephilim Homeowners Association, who kept squawking about the ark causing a marked decline in neighborhood property values.) According to Genesis 7:10, the waters came seven days after everyone and everything was onboard, safe and secure with the hatches well–battened down.

As a community of believers, Noah had a pretty good crew. While they prepared for this ominous event, they reflected on the Lord's promises. They prayed and did everything He asked with a willing spirit, in spite of the bruises, cuts, and hammered thumbs. And while enduring the voyage, they lived and worked in a spirit of obedience and faith. For instruction and encouragement, they had the Lord and they had their family—to share their needs, concerns, victories, and failures. Worship was not strictly a ritual or a Sunday morning event to attend for entertainment. Worship was life, with God at the center.

Hang On—It's Raining!

> On the seventeenth day of the second month—on that day all the springs of the great deep burst forth, and the floodgates of the heavens were opened. And rain fell on the earth forty days and forty nights (7:11–12).

Or as we might sing from the song of another great maritime crisis:

> The weather started getting rough
> The tiny ship was tossed;
> If not for the courage of the fearless crew,
> The Minnow would be lost; the Minnow would be lost.

—*The Ballad of Gilligan's Island*

To gain some perspective on the amount of rain that created the Flood, here is a possible scenario. If the rain had fallen at an unprecedented 36 inches per hour, forty full days of 24–hour torrent would have created approximately 34,560 inches or 2,880 feet of water. This is certainly substantial but not globally inundating. A medium–sized mountain like Pike's Peak (14,100 feet) would still have been 11,200 feet above water. But we know that the waters rose until the entire world was awash. The highest mountains were at least twenty feet under water (see 7:20). So where did all the water come from? Geological and archaeological studies have indicated that massive seismic activity could have precipitated unprecedented flooding. If huge underground rivers, lakes, and "springs of the deep" were released, combined with storms that generated more rain, the water level would have risen to epic proportions. Rainfall at 36 inches per hour would send the average person swimming after only two hours—and keep them swimming for another 958 hours without stopping! Even Navy Seals would have found this impossible.

I can imagine neighbors and maybe a few relatives sloshing through the rising tide to get to Noah's floating barn. By the time of the Flood, Methuselah and Lamech were dead, as were most of Noah's direct ancestors, but others who had made fun of Noah and his faith in God pleaded desperately for rescue as the waters crept higher and higher. Did Noah and his family sing songs of praise to God to buoy their faith or to drown out the din of the rain and the wails of the drowning? The thankful family kept busy, no doubt, as they rode out God's "perfect storm." Animals had to be fed, cows needed to be milked, and lots of hay had to be changed in the stalls so the smell would not be overwhelming! How did the predators stay content without being served what lay in the adjoining stall for dinner? If I had been bunked next to the large carnivores, I would have slept with one eye open, just in case.

The Wait after Docking

While the residents of God's floating menagerie were safely tucked in bed, "every living thing on the face of the earth was wiped out. . . . Only Noah was left, and those with him in the ark. The waters flooded the earth for 150 days" (7:23–24). By the end of the 150 days, five months into the voyage, Noah and crew must have longed to walk on dry land again. Did they think God had forgotten where they were? *Will we ever get off this maritime farm?* God didn't forget them for a moment. He stopped the rains and plugged up the springs and sent a strong wind to begin to dry up the water.

After bobbing around for what seemed like an eternity, the ark came to a grinding halt on the mountains of Ararat in what is now Turkey. It would still take some time before the ground was dry enough for the ark's inhabitants to see land (see 8:4–5), but each day brought encouragement that the flood was subsiding. They just had to be patient and wait. Patience, however, is something we have historically had in short supply. We know what we want, at least we think we do, and we want it now. We want our desires met as quickly as possible, and we especially hate to wait for the Lord, although that is exactly what He expects us to do to demonstrate obedience and faith.

Forty days after running aground, Noah popped the hatch to take a look. He sent out a raven hoping there might be some dry land for it to land on. But alas, the poor bird could just circle until its wings grew tired. Noah then sent out a dove to see if the waters had receded enough. Like the raven, the dove could not find a place to land. Noah waited another week before he sent the dove out again. This time it returned with a fresh, green olive leaf in its mouth. Trees! After one more week the dove went out again, but never came back. Maybe the aroma of unwashed humans and animals made it want nothing more to do with the project (see 8:6–12). The entire process from Flood to disembarkment took 375 days—just over a year.

Shortly after Noah celebrated his 601st birthday, the water was gone, and the Lord told them to come out and begin new lives. They unloaded the animals—or rather opened the door and got out of their way. Were Noah's boys assigned the task of cleaning up after the animals were gone? Did the family live in the ark, trailer–park style, until they could build a more permanent dwelling? Once they stretched their legs and perhaps rolled in the grass for the first time in over a year, Noah took some of the animals that had been traveling with them and offered a sacrifice to God in worship and thanksgiving. Remembering the old stories about Cain and Abel, he performed the sacrifice to show that he considered his relationship with God to be paramount. As the smoke of the sacrifice wafted upward, the Lord saw Noah's heartfelt obedience, and He was pleased, further renewing His promise to "never again . . . destroy all living creatures, as I have done" (8:21).

Basic Rules to Live By

When God blessed Noah's family, He again ordered them to "be fruitful and increase in number" (9:1). Everything was given to them for food, just as it had been with Adam and Eve—except they were not to eat meat with blood still in it. God was reminding them of the fact that life is in blood, and life is precious. He did not force them to become vegetarians, but He wanted them to have such reverence for life that blood would not be a part of the meal. Blood carried yet another significance—reminding them that God would not tolerate another Cain–and–Abel episode. If someone took the life of another, they would have to give an accounting with their own. Not only was this decree necessary for civil rule, but also to demonstrate the extraordinary value that man needed to place on human life, for it is created in the "image of God" (see 9:5–6).

The Lord established a covenant with Noah and all his descendants, bestowing the rainbow as a sign of that pledge (see 9:12–16). Unfortunately, it did not take long for Noah's family to let their relationship with God slide, as dysfunction seeped in again.

Chapter 5

Products of Dysfunction

Can't They Get It Right?

Sometimes sin derives from curiosity, from looking in places where we should not look or by experimenting with increasing dangers and thrills. In most cases, though, sin evolves from a slow, downward spiral of considering the things of God to be of little or no significance or value. No one wakes up in the morning and adds "defy God" to their To Do list. Sin is usually less deliberate, but nonetheless inevitable. Sin happens—because our fallen, human nature instinctively chooses to do wrong. That is why parents have to teach their children to tell the truth and share their toys and show good manners—because lying, selfishness, and disrespect all come naturally.

Such was the case with Noah and his family. They had survived the flood and offered sacrifice with thanksgiving. They had witnessed first-hand the mighty force of God's wrath on those who systematically sin against Him and the sustaining power of God's mercy on those who serve Him. And they had moved on with their lives. Noah was a farmer in pre–Flood days before he became God's sailor. So when dry land was available again, he planted a vineyard—and that's when the trouble began. Perhaps after so long on the ark, Noah was sick of water and found wine a pleasant change of pace. But Noah overdid it and got drunk. He got really loaded.

Often, what is a good thing in moderation becomes harmful when taken to excess. Maybe he was happy, celebrating life and a good harvest away from the confines of the ark. Maybe he forgot that this vintage had a real kick to it. We don't know. Noah may have been hot from the wine, the climate, or both. What we do know is that he was blitzed and ended up in his tent naked and probably passed out (see 9:21).

Ham, the youngest son, found his dad sprawled in the tent and went to tell his brothers. The brothers came in and, seeing their father vulnerable, covered him up. In fact, out of respect they laid a robe over him with their faces turned away so they would not see him. Noah awoke and, noticing himself awkwardly dressed, knew something was amiss. Questioning the boys, he discovered what Ham had done and was furious to the point of cursing Ham and his descendants: "Cursed be Canaan! The lowest of slaves will he be to his brothers" (9:25).

Almost with the next breath Noah blessed the other sons: "Blessed be the Lord, the God of Shem! May Canaan be the slave of Shem. May God extend the territory of Japheth; may Japheth live in the tents of Shem, and may Canaan be his slave" (9:26–27). Why was Noah so mad?

Ham thought it was a big joke. He did not show respect for his father or understand that Noah's condition resulted from an error in judgment. Ham should have shown greater sympathy. Instead, he held his father—the one who had made it possible for them to be alive—up to ridicule and disgrace. Ham demonstrated such lack of character by finding pleasure at his father's expense and, in so doing, revealed one of the true marks of a dysfunctional family or community—the instinct to shame. By changing the focus from the action to the person, it was as if Ham had said, "It is not your drunkenness that was bad, but you, Noah. You are worthless as a father and as a family leader. You are unworthy of respect."

Had this character trait of mankind become so inbred that even the Flood could not eradicate it? And if Noah was made to appear unworthy of respect, then his God, by extension, could also appear to be of little or no significance or value. See how the downward spiral begins? Perhaps this is why the Lord gave Moses the Ten Commandments, where, after stating the primacy of our relationship with God, the next most significant behavior must be to honor and respect our parents.

Playing Favorites

Even if Noah had every right to be angry and express his displeasure with Ham, he only compounded the problem. Noah displayed another signature trait of dysfunctional families by favoring Seth and Japheth over their brother. By elevating them to a place of honor above Ham, he planted seeds of discontent, rivalry, and hatred that would bear sour fruit for thousands of years. Throughout Middle Eastern history, the descendants of Seth, the Jews, would be perpetually at odds with the descendants of Ham, Israel's enemy. (Genesis clearly identifies Ham with Canaan—the country that created problems for Israel.) Nowhere does Scripture indicate that Ham sought his father's forgiveness; neither does it indicate that Noah offered it. After such a promising new beginning, the family unit was again split into adversaries when they should have been allies.

Noah died at 950 as the last of the aged patriarchs. We don't know if he ever got drunk again, but I doubt it, given the trouble it caused the first time. If he did learn his lesson, apparently he was the only one.

The Shame Game Continues

Over the years, some have maladapted Noah's curse to defend the mistreatment of certain nations or ethnic groups. Still others see this long–standing situation of hostility as punishment for Noah's use of alcohol. Both interpretations seem to be missing the point, while repeating the dysfunctional habit of adding shame and blame to their thinking. Perhaps those so quick to accuse should take this lesson to heart and begin to base their faith and relationship with God on who they are in Him—as opposed to what they "don't do."

Sometime after the wine incident, Noah's three boys went their separate ways and continued to build their own families as they sought their own positions in the world. These three branches of Noah's family spread out for many generations, making connections and intermarriages to repopulate the earth after the Flood. Being from one family, however, they shared a common lineage and language. Brother Shem, the eldest, did well living in the hill country of what would be modern Iran and Iraq. Not much is known about Japheth, the middle child, but of the three, Ham's family seems to have been the most prosperous.

Despite the curse, one of his descendants went on to found an empire. Nimrod, a great warrior, built great cities in Babylon, Shinar, and Nineveh. Ham was also the ancestor of many of the "ites"—the Hittites, Jebusites, Amorites, Girgashites, Hivites, Arkites, Sinites, Arvadites, Zemarites, and Hamathites. The residents of Sodom and Gomorrah, and eventually the Philistines (many of whom were enemies of the Jews), also descended from Ham (see 10:9–20). One of these clans moved east and settled in the plain of Shinar. They had little use for the God of Noah or any other deity who did not suit their liking. No longer nomads living in sheepskin tents, they built houses of baked bricks with tar for mortar.

The Tower of Babel

At some unspecified point in their development, the clan from Shinar decided to embark on an unprecedented building campaign, which became the city of Babel: "Come, let us build ourselves a city, with a tower that reaches to the heavens, so that we may make a name for ourselves and not be scattered over the face of the whole earth" (11:4). The aim, however, was not to build a tower to reach heaven in order to see God and worship Him. It was to look in and verify that He wasn't there at all. The citizens of Babel, originators of secular humanism, wanted to deify man, not God. If they could prove there was no God, they would tout themselves as the supreme creative force in the universe. They were eager to promote this concept and more than willing to risk cutting themselves adrift from the Lord in order to proclaim their findings and ridicule any of God's faithful followers.

God can truly be understood as "our heavenly Father" in this situation because He was parenting some headstrong children. Kids have exasperated their parents in every age, and the children of Babel were no different. "The Lord came down to see the city and the tower that the men were building . . . [and] said, 'If as one people speaking the same language they have begun to do this, then nothing they plan to do will be impossible for them'" (11:5–6).

The Lord decided to confuse Babel's language so the people could not understand each other. This certainly made things more difficult and stopped the construction of the tower—and the city. (It must have been quite a challenge for the construction foreman not to have his workers understand what he was saying.) Some groups were still able to communicate effectively with each other—or else they would all have resorted to grunts, hand gestures, and funny noises. The members of Babel's fragmented society then gravitated to those they could understand and who understood them, scattering themselves to different areas in the process. As people moved apart, God knew there would be less potential for rebellion against Him. There is power in numbers, after all.

Does our society obey any better than the people of Babel, as we push our own will and deny God in spite of His care? And even though we speak the same language in our immediate worlds, we still have a nearly insurmountable problem communicating with our spouses, our children, our friends and co–workers. We get angry and yell and we are often unheard and misunderstood. This deficiency in mankind's mental wiring also makes it extraordinarily difficult to share the good news of God's grace. So we resort to small talk about weather or sports. Thanks to the mess at Babel, we seem condemned never to express the deep longings of our hearts and souls, until that loss drives home our need to communicate with God—the only One who truly hears and understands even the deep groans and sighs too painful to put into words.

What the Lord confused at Babel, however, He corrected with the giving of the Holy Spirit at Pentecost as recorded in Acts 2:1–12. On that day, rather than hearing cacophony and the result of dysfunction, the people heard the life–changing gospel preached in their own language without the aid of translators. The Lord proved that He was still in charge. In that regard, it appears true that the more things change, the more they stay the same, however advanced we may think we are.

Chapter 6

Abraham

A Faithful Man and a Mighty Promise

From Adam and Eve through the episode at Babel, the account in the Book of Genesis has chronicled the origins of the human family. In the story of Abraham we see the beginnings of the family of God and the founding of the nation of Israel. With very few exceptions, each member of the Genesis families is marked with sin, as played out in their behavior, taking them down from mythic proportions and placing them among the ranks of the dysfunctional, just like us. But if you were to look at a theological dictionary under the word "faith," it might say, "see Abraham" (see Hebrews 11).

The Abrahamic saga began in the city of Ur in Chaldea (what is now southern Iraq). Things did not follow suddenly after the incident at Babel the way time passes in a Hollywood movie. Time is not compressed into a few minutes or a simple "meanwhile back at the ranch." In this case the "meanwhile" covered ten generations over a span of many years, for although these people lived much longer than we do today, lifespans were decreasing. No one knows what caused the decline—exposure to thermonuclear radiation, new diseases, or perhaps having more children and relatives. One theory espouses the idea that the Flood depleted the protective atmosphere that was created at Eden. Increased exposure to the sun would certainly increase the risk of cancer and the mortality rate (see Genesis 11:10–26).

Abram's father, Terah, was a descendant of the Semitic line of Noah's eldest son, Shem, through ten generations (see 11:10–26). Terah was the catalyst who placed Abram in the right place to be selected God's man for the future. Genesis 11:27 says, "This is the account of Terah. Terah became the father of Abram, Nahor, and Haran. And Haran became the father of Lot." Haran, after having a city named after him, died soon thereafter in Ur. Little is known of him. The account centers on Abram and his nephew Lot.

Abram's wife Sarai, whose name means "princess," also figures prominently in the tale. We don't know how long Abram and Sarai were married; we do know they were childless. Scripture makes that point clear, saying it two ways in the same sentence: "Now Sarai was barren; she had no children" (11:30). Why does the Bible stress this point? Many couples today have no children either by choice or by circumstance, but having children was a big deal when lineage, genealogy, and transference of tribal authority were far more important than they are now.

One day Terah packed up his son Abram, his grandson Lot, and his daughter–in–law Sarai and set out from the great city of Ur to rural Canaan. The Bible does not indicate that this was the Lord's plan for Terah or explain what prompted him to relocate. They just struck out— but traveled only as far as the city of Haran and settled there. I imagine that Terah, after traveling this distance with the family, arrived in Haran and decided to take a permanent break. Terah later died in Haran at the age of 205, leaving Abram head of the household—far from Ur and nowhere near Canaan.

"Are We There Yet?"

We don't know exactly how long Abram lived in the city of Haran—probably long enough to learn a trade, accumulate a semblance of affluence, make a name for himself, and be recognized by God as someone special. One day, the Lord called to Abram to share the first part of His master plan for this simple man of faith: "Leave your country, your people and your father's household and go to the land I will show you" (12:1). In one breath God said move, without telling Abram where; in the next breath God made wonderful, sweeping promises: "I will make you into a great nation and I will bless you; I will make your name great, and you will be a blessing. I will bless those who bless you, and whoever curses you I will curse; and all peoples on earth will be blessed through you" (12:2–3).

I have moved many times in my life, but never with a promise like that. But then again, I have always known where I was going before I left. It made it easier to get my mail that way. But strangely enough, Abram did just as he was told. If it had been me, I would have liked to know where I was going and, at the very least, fill out a change–of–address form at the post office. Abram had no such reservations. His thinking was that the Lord would take care of everything. Abram just left town with his wife and nephew and waited for the Lord to give them a nudge in the right direction. And for those who think they are too old to make a major life change, Abram was seventy–five years old when this adventure began. He and his family took their possessions and headed for the land of Canaan (12:4–5).

When they finally reached Canaan by the great tree of Moreh in Shechem (apparently a well-known landmark), the Lord said, "We're here!" In relieved response, Abram built an altar and worshipped the Lord, giving thanks for their safe arrival in their new home. In fact, he built several altars, including another at Bethel where they camped (12:6–8). Being a nomadic herdsman, Abram explored the surrounding area. He wandered south toward the Negev, constantly looking for pasture and fresh water. After a time, there was a great famine.

Here Abram's family's story begins to unravel just a bit. Up to this point, he had trusted God in all things and had distinguished himself above all his relatives and neighbors as a man of faith. But then Abram took matters into his own hands—with nearly disastrous consequences. Because food was scarce, Abram and Sarai made the relatively short hike to Egypt, planning to remain there until the famine was over. It was then that Abram let his trust in the Lord slip, joining the ranks of the dysfunctional Genesis family as a liar.

A Moment of Panic

As the couple was preparing to submit to Egyptian customs and immigration inspection, Abram recalled all the horror stories he had heard about travelers in the land of the Pharaohs. Abram was afraid that if the rulers knew that beautiful Sarai was his wife, they would simply have Abram eliminated in order to add her to one of their harems. Abram told Sarai, "Say you are my sister, so that I will be treated well for your sake and my life will be spared because of you" (12:13).

Sure enough, when Pharaoh's officials saw that Sarai was gorgeous, she was invited to Pharaoh's palace. Scripture does not say that Pharaoh formally married Abram's "sister," but only that Pharaoh took care of them and was extremely generous, giving them gifts of livestock and servants. Was this Pharaoh's usual way of being kind to strangers from Canaan, or was this some sort of dowry to be paid to Sarai's family through Abram? (12:14–16). Why else would Pharaoh treat wandering shepherds so extravagantly?

All was well, or so they thought. Pharaoh had a new love interest. Sarai was safe and well fed during the famine. Abram was amassing wealth that would hold the family in good stead when they returned to Canaan one day. They may have thought, *Surely the Lord has His hand in this. Why else would this plan come together so perfectly?* But it was not God's plan. It was not the truth, and there was no way God was going to bless their deception any more than He will bless ours. Just because things seem to work out all right for a time, don't think God has forgotten.

Scripture says the Lord "inflicted serious diseases on Pharaoh and his household because of Abram's wife Sarai" (12:17). It doesn't say what the diseases were except to intimate they were serious or painful. Pharaoh didn't take long to determine that these maladies came as punishment for some terrifically serious sin. Perhaps he traced the outbreak of the afflictions back in time and discovered that they started soon after Abram and Sarai came to Egypt.

Sometimes Scripture cannot adequately capture tone of voice. It simply says that Pharaoh "summoned" Abram to the palace. I don't think it was a casual invitation, and certainly not one to be ignored. "What have you done to me?" Pharaoh demanded. "Why didn't you tell me she was your wife? Why did you say, 'She is my sister,' so that I took her to be my wife? Now then, here is your wife. Take her and go!" (12:18–19). There is no explanation or excuse from Abram and

Sarai, and Scripture gives no additional comment except to state that Pharaoh had them both deported. Abram and Sarai had officially worn out their welcome (12:20). But it could have been much worse. Abram and Sarai could have "disappeared" into the Egyptian desert—never to be seen again.

A Wise Choice

Because of his faith and obedience, Abram would become the father of nations; he would be blessed and be the means of blessing to others. Anyone who hindered, harmed, or cursed him in any way would get the same treatment back from the Lord. Throughout the whole "sister" deception, however, Abram had exhibited the belief that truth was pliable enough to be bent to suit his own ends. Lies would become part of the family heritage, in fact. Abram had lied to save his life, or so he thought. Several generations later, grandson Jacob would make lying his primary claim to fame.

Abram must have done well for himself in Egypt, since he came away "very wealthy in livestock and in silver and gold" (13:2). Rich and considered a high roller by anyone's standards, he could return to the land of Canaan and live in whatever style passed for luxury in those days. So, Abram and Sarai moved with Lot and all their herds and their servants back to Bethel—the place Abram had settled when he first came to Canaan. There this huge company tried to make a home without getting in each other's way. But the land could not support them all, and quarreling began between the two families and the Canaanites who still lived in the area and were getting squeezed out.

Abram told Lot that he didn't want any "bad blood" between them. He said, "Let's part company. If you go to the left, I'll go to the right; if you go to the right, I'll go to the left" (13:8–9). Generously Abram divided the land and gave Lot first pick of what he wanted. (Mothers have a variation on this theme. When dividing a candy bar or a piece of cake between children, one child makes the cut, but the other gets first pick of the pieces. That way, the end result is equitable for both parties.) Perhaps Abram was learning. God had taken care of him before and would do so again regardless of where his family settled. It was best to tell the truth from the start and not become entangled in a mess like the Egypt fiasco. If this was the case, then Abram was the first since Enoch and Noah in this multi–generational family of dysfunctionals who thought of someone other than himself.

Seeing that the plain of the Jordan River was well watered and fertile, much like old accounts of the Garden of Eden, Lot chose the best looking property, leaving Abram with the more remote wilderness of Canaan. Unfortunately, Lot made his decision purely on ease of management without first checking the cities to see what they were like. Lot and Abram shook hands, wished each other well, parted company, and moved on to their new homes—Abram to the hill country and Lot to the twin cities of Sodom and Gomorrah (see 13:10-12). We will soon see how wrong Lot's choice was.

Abram must have wondered if this land was indeed his final destination—the place to call his own, where he would not have to keep moving. As soon as Lot had left, the Lord reaffirmed His promise that good things would accompany Abram's faithfulness.

> Lift up your eyes from where you are and look north and south, east and west. All the land that you see I will give to you and your offspring forever. I will make your offspring like the dust of the earth, so that if anyone could count the dust, then your offspring could be counted. Go, walk through the length and breadth of the land, for I am giving it to you (13:14–17).

It must have seemed a bit overwhelming for Abram to become the father of a population too great in number to count, considering that he and his wife were childless. To be the owner of all the land he could see was a gift beyond description! Abram did well when he stayed close to the Lord; he only had problems when he steered away from the plan. We make the same mistake. When we feel blessed and favored, we begin to believe that we know what we're doing and that we can create our own agendas to suit our immediate needs—because we deserve it, and God could use our help. Wrong!

Abram to the Rescue

Sodom was not much of a city by our modern standards, but shops, restaurants, and theaters provided some culture and diversion to residents and tourists. Oh, and another thing—Sodom was also the capital city of perversion. Every deviant sexual practice was not only available but encouraged. And Lot and his family were living right in the middle of it. I wonder if he later considered his choice of real estate to be yet another case of "it seemed like a good idea at the time."

As bad as the moral situation was in Sodom, the city's political stability was no better. Scripture says that a union of five kings went to war with an alliance of four other kings that included the kings of Sodom and Gomorrah. During the battle and the taking of Sodom, Gomorrah, and the surrounding area, Lot, along with his family and all their food and possessions, was captured (14:1–12). One member of Lot's party escaped and ran to tell Uncle Abram the grim news. By this time, Abram was a major landholder with influence so that when Abram spoke, people listened. Abram assembled 318 fighting men from his extended family and servants and rushed to Lot's aid. They chased the raiders all night long and managed to defeat them, rescuing the captives and recovering all of the stolen loot (14:13–15). This brave escapade further enhanced Abram's reputation in the community.

The Seeds of a Theocracy

"After Abram returned from defeating Kedorlaomer and the kings allied with him, the king of Sodom came out to meet him" (14:17), as did Melchizedek, the king of Salem and "the priest of God Most High." As both a king and priest, Melchizedek is considered a prototype of Jesus as King and great High Priest, worthy of tithes and worship. He, too, was one without beginning or end since there was no record of his birth or death or lineage. Even the name "Melchizedek" speaks of Jesus Christ as "king of righteousness" and "king of peace" (see Hebrews 6:20, 7:2–4).

Melchizedek brought out bread and wine, and he blessed Abram with these words: "Blessed be Abram by God Most High, Creator of heaven and earth. And blessed be God Most High, who delivered your enemies into your hand" (Genesis 14:19–20). The king must have made quite an impression on Abram, since the very next phrase in Scripture states that Abram "gave him a tenth of everything" (14:20). Abram gave

Melchizedek a tithe of all his possessions—an offering customarily reserved for God alone. Nothing indicates that this offering was required or even expected, except that Melchizedek spoke on behalf of the One who had promised Abram a home, an inheritance, and a grand posterity. God had never failed him, and Abram may have felt the Lord had been with him in battle, as well, since he had been successful at liberating Lot and the others from their captors.

Not wanting to be left out of the victory celebrations, the king of Sodom chimed in, "Give me the people [prisoners] and keep the goods for yourself" (14:21). Perhaps the king wanted to pay Abram for performing such a valuable service, while claiming some of the credit for the rescue. But Abram replied that he had taken an oath to the Lord not to accept any compensation for his efforts other than the food his men had eaten during the campaign (14:22–24). So the king of Sodom watched helplessly as a tenth of the spoils of battle were dedicated to the Lord's service and made as an offering to God. The Lord was working through Abram to grow a theocracy that would forever change religion and faith around the world. With the offering made and accepted, Melchizedek vanished as suddenly as he had appeared.

Chapter 7

Abram and Sarai

Short–Circuiting God's Plan

The Lord continued to show His abundant patience with Abram, reassuring him not to be afraid and reminding him of the strength and confidence that follows faith: "I am your shield, your very great reward" (15:1). But Abram still felt insecure, despite all his wealth and recent stability, namely because he was childless. He worried about having to leave all he had worked so hard to obtain to a household servant, Eliezer of Damascus (see 15:2–3). We all know that "family treasures," the bronzed baby shoes, the photo albums, the items of sentimental value, are likely to appear as junk to anyone outside the family.

First, the Good News . . . Then, the Bad

In a vision the Lord said to Abram that Eliezer would not be his heir; a son "coming from your own body will be your heir" (15:4). To further illustrate His point, the Lord took Abram outside and had him look into the night sky. God told Abram that his descendants would be as numerous as the stars (15:5). Abram accepted God at His word, and the Lord credited that faith, as simple as it was, as righteousness.

After the Lord and Abram sealed this solemn pledge with animal sacrifices, God revealed the ominous prophecy of those descendants, as "a thick and dreadful darkness" befell Abram: "Your descendants will be strangers in a country not their own, and they will be enslaved and mistreated 400 years" (15:12–13). But there was also more good news.

To Abram's descendants God gave the land that stretches from the river of Egypt to the Euphrates River. They would inherit great wealth, while the nation that enslaved them would be punished. God further promised that Abram would live to an old age and would rest in peace long before any of this misfortune occurred (see 15:14–15,18).

Sarai's Plan

There are times when we all would like God to move a little faster. When the Lord seems to be taking too long to make things happen, our impatience tempts us to take matters into our own hands and do what we think is right to resolve the problem. When we do, we usually make the wrong choice in the wrong way—and with the worst possible result. Such was the case for the childless Abram and Sarai.

Sarai decided to jump start God's plan of making descendants by suggesting that Abram have sexual relations with her Egyptian maidservant Hagar: "Perhaps I can build a family through her" (16:2). Abram agreed, and when Hagar successfully conceived, Abram and Sarai were on their way to having a family and heir, but not the way God had promised.

When Hagar became pregnant (and undoubtedly favored and pampered), she began to ridicule and "despise her mistress" (16:4). Did Hagar mock Sarai for her supposed inability to have children? This is quite probable, especially if Hagar was one of the slaves given to Abram when he left Egypt. In those days, being without offspring was a social stigma of the greatest magnitude, and Hagar wanted to demonstrate her superiority over Sarai.

This attitude from Hagar provoked Sarai to shout angrily at Abram, "You are responsible for the wrong I am suffering. I put my servant in your arms, and now that she knows she is pregnant, she despises me. May the Lord judge between you and me" (16:5).

Abram replied, "Your servant is in your hands. . . . Do with her whatever you think best" (16:6). So Sarai mistreated Hagar until Hagar ran away.

The Bible's account of the conversation between husband and wife sounds so matter-of-fact, but I imagine the exchange was considerably more heated. The entire encampment must have overheard their argument, as accusations and counter–accusations flew back and forth with increasing volume and intensity. A celebrity pregnancy is not something that can be kept secret very long, especially when it involves the patriarch of the tribe, his wife, and his wife's maid. A likely excerpt from the dialogue in the Abram–of–Ur household during those days might have been the following:

> SARAI: This is all your fault, Abram. We should have stayed in Ur instead of hauling everything all this way, and for what? A promise from God to make an old goat like you father of nations, and me the mother? How ridiculous is that? I went along with the move thing, and even suggested having a child for you by Hagar, but now I am the laughing stock of the tribe. Hagar flaunts herself in front of me every day—and what do you do? Nothing. Well, I've had enough. Either she goes, Mr. Father–of–Many–Nations, or I go! And God have mercy on you if you make the wrong choice!

This level of marital discord had not been reflected in the Bible since Adam and Eve were banished from the Garden. Abram's reply was the typical male response in times of crisis. Rather than taking charge of the situation by reassuring Sarai that she was his true love and would be until they grew ancient together, he ducked the issue. He could have said, "Sarai, remember when we went to Egypt and I said you were my sister? I did that not out of fear for my own safety, but because I loved you so much. I could not bear the thought of losing you. You are the one for me—forever and always." *He could have said that.* But instead, he said, "Do with her whatever you think best." Abram's choice was to make *no* choice—and to drop the situation back into Sarai's lap.

This family scenario—in which the wife gets angry while looking for reassurance and security of true love, as the husband becomes more and more withdrawn—illustrates several aspects of dysfunctionality in people. The sad commentary is that families have repeated it over and over again for centuries.

From Abram to Abraham

When the abuse was no longer bearable, Hagar ran away from her mistress. The angel of the Lord found her all alone by a desert spring along the road to Shur, out in the middle of nowhere. When the angel asked Hagar to explain *both* her comings and goings, Hagar could only speak of where she had been. Perhaps she had no destination, no plan, and was merely fleeing. The angel told her, "'Go back to your mistress and submit to her.' The angel added, 'I will so increase your descendants that they will be too numerous to count. . . . You will have a son. You shall name him Ishmael, for the Lord has heard of your misery'" (16:9–11). But the angel added a promise that would come as a shock to any prospective mother, for it spoke of difficulty and sounded more like a curse than a blessing: "He will be a wild donkey of a man; his hand will be against everyone and everyone's hand against him, and he will live in hostility toward all his brothers" (16:12).

In thanks for the promise of her son, Hagar gave this name to the Lord who spoke to her: "You are the God who sees me" (16:13). Even though Ishmael and Hagar were not the chosen ones, God saw their plight and made a place for them. In due course, Hagar gave birth to Ishmael as promised. Abram was eighty–six years old (16:15–16).

The narrative then takes a thirteen–year leap to where the Lord is finally going to bring His promise of an heir to completion. "When Abram was ninety–nine years old, the Lord appeared to him and said, 'I am God Almighty; walk before Me and be blameless. I will confirm My covenant between Me and you and will greatly increase your numbers'" (17:1–2).

Imagine all that happens to a person or family in thirteen years. Ishmael could have been a freshman in high school, and if he had been like every other teen that has *ever* been, he would have known everything and had an opinion on all of it. The lad would have been quite a handful—a handful and a formidable rival.

When Abram received this confirmation that Sarai would have a child, he did what any rational person would do when confronted by the Almighty Himself—he fell on his face and worshipped God. And he also kept his mouth shut to Sarai. Abram had lived with the Ishmael experiment and was more than willing to do it God's way this time.

Reminded again of the covenant with God, Abram was given a name change worthy of the event to take place:

> No longer will you be called Abram; your name will be Abraham, for I have made you a father of many nations. I will make you very fruitful; I will make nations of you, and kings will come from you. I will establish My covenant as an everlasting covenant between Me and you and your descendants after you for the generations to come, to be your God and the God of your descendants after you (17:4–7).

When the Lord adds to a person's character, He often changes his or her name, the new name being symbolic of a new ministry and effectiveness for service. Cephas, whose name means "pebble," became Peter the "rock." After his conversion, Saul, oppressor of the Christian church, became Paul, Christianity's greatest writer and church planter. But it appears that God also wanted some means of showing a tangible expression of participation in His covenantal relationship with Abraham and his legacy. God then said to Abraham:

> Every male among you shall be circumcised. . . . It will be the sign of the covenant between Me and you. For the generations to come every male among you who is eight days old must be circumcised, including those born in your household or bought with money from a foreigner—those who are not your offspring. . . . My covenant in your flesh is to be an everlasting covenant. Any uncircumcised male . . . will be cut off from his people; he has broken My covenant (17:10–14).

The sign sealing the covenant needed to be something that once done, could not be undone without great pain and difficulty. Documents can be altered or forged. Anything designed by man, with or without the use of a computer, can be changed, deleted, or faked. But circumcision cannot be concealed.

Apparently circumcision was not yet a common practice among the Middle Eastern people of that time. Therefore, the nationality and religious affiliation of a Hebrew would be obvious. (During the later Greek and Roman periods when athletes competed unclad, the affiliation with the descendants of Abraham could not be hidden at all.) In obedience to the plan of God and without reservation or further delay, Abraham, age ninety–nine, and Ishmael, age thirteen, and every male of their household submitted to circumcision as God instructed (see 17:23–27). All men were humbled in this way as they began their relationship with Jehovah—equal to one another in heritage, in obedience, in discomfort.

The Lord also had news for Sarai. Her name was to be changed to Sarah—a more suitable name for the mother of nations and kings, for God promised Abraham a son by her (17:15–16). To this reminder, Abraham had to laugh as he fell facedown again. But also worried about the prospect of learning how to change diapers, do around–the–clock feedings, toilet train, and survive the "terrible twos," Abraham wondered, "'Will a son be born to a man a hundred years old? Will Sarah bear a child at the age of ninety?' And Abraham said to God, 'If only Ishmael might live under your blessing!'" (17:17–18). God replied:

> Your wife Sarah will bear you a son, and you will call him Isaac. I will establish My covenant with him as an ever-lasting covenant for his descendants after him. And as for Ishmael, I have heard you: I will surely bless him; I will make him fruitful and will greatly increase his numbers. He will be the father of twelve rulers, and I will make him into a great nation. But My covenant I will establish with Isaac, whom Sarah will bear to you by this time next year (17:19–21).

Every time Abraham tried to counter with a "yes, but" the Lord reminded him of what was going to happen. God keeps His word in His way, in His time—even to a dad–to–be at one hundred! God even had the name picked out, as He does quite often. Zechariah was struck dumb until he told people that his little boy would be named John—the child who grew to be John the Baptizer. And to Mary and Joseph—"You are to give Him the name Jesus, because He will save His people from their sins" (Matthew 1:21). One can only wonder what was going on in Abraham's mind—this father of nations, ancestor of kings, and expectant parent of a crying, demanding infant.

The Apostle Paul, writing to the church in Galatia, used the examples of Abraham, Sarah, Isaac, Ishmael, and Hagar to explain the difference between living under a heavy–handed law and living with the liberating grace of God. Paul compared man's relationship to the law as one of slavery—a relationship based on duties and obligations, as Hagar and Ishmael had with Abraham. By contrast, He compared man's relationship to God's grace as one of freedom—a family connection with full rights of inheritance as sons and daughters, which Sarah and Isaac had with Abraham.

Chapter 8

Melt the Ice, Harden the Clay

Gain a Son, Lose a City

The Lord contacted Abraham once again while the old patriarch was seated in front of his tent in the shade of the great trees of Mamre. Abraham looked up and saw three men who had not been there just moments before. In this neighborhood of family and friends, the sudden presence of strangers would certainly be cause for surprise. But in this case, these angelic beings did not have a chance to give the customary greeting of "Fear not," as they always did when they appeared from nowhere, scaring people half to death. As soon as Abraham saw them, he hurried to meet them, bowing low to the ground.

Welcoming them, he provided water to wash their feet (18:2–5). They agreed to stay awhile, and Abraham rushed off to find Sarah. Nothing like Sarah's delicious bread, hot from the oven, to make a good impression. Just to make sure they were well fed, he ran to the herd and personally selected a calf to be prepared for dinner, which they ate with curds and milk (18:6–8). While they were eating, the visitors asked, "Where is your wife Sarah?" (18:9). Abraham indicated that she was in the family tent nearby. Then the angel of the Lord restated the promise of a son and heir. He informed Abraham that Sarah would have her baby upon His return the following year.

Thinking herself safe from detection, Sarah chuckled at the thought of becoming a mother at her age. She thought it hilarious—

the angel did not. He asked Abraham, "Why did Sarah laugh? . . . Is anything too hard for the Lord? I will return to you at the appointed time next year and Sarah will have a son" (18:13–14).

Sarah was afraid. *How could he have heard me laugh unless he was truly sent by God?* When confronted, she lied. But the angelic visitors insisted, "You most certainly did laugh, and you know we heard it" (see 18:15). So, Abraham and Sarah's son would be named Isaac—son of laughter—to remind both parents of their cynical attitude. They were learning, though, that the Lord can and will accomplish what He sets out to do—with or without our cooperation. He prefers, however, that we are willing.

God's Final Offer

As the angels prepared to leave, they discussed among themselves if they should brief Abraham on the more pressing mission that brought them. If, indeed, he was a great man of God, Abraham had a right to know what was going to happen: Sodom and Gomorrah, having reached new depths of depravity, would be destroyed. So as Abraham was blessed for his faithfulness, Sodom and Gomorrah were to be blasted for their lack of it. The two angelic visitors went on to Sodom and Gomorrah to reconnoiter the situation, while Abraham remained to speak to the angel of the Lord:

> Will You sweep away the righteous with the wicked? What if there are fifty righteous people in the city? Will You really sweep it away and not spare the place for the sake of the fifty righteous people in it? Far be it from You to do such a thing—to kill the righteous with the wicked, treating the righteous and the wicked alike. . . . Will not the Judge of all the earth do right? (18:23–25)

Abraham was taking quite a risk telling God what was the right thing to do, since Abraham had his own history of stretching the truth and taking matters into his own hands. But appreciating Abraham's passionate appeal, the Lord agreed to spare the city if fifty righteous people could be found (see 18:26). Despite God's need to stamp out wickedness with great severity and finality, He is always eager to be gracious, not wishing to punish the undeserving. God even provides for the righteous to the point that the wicked are blessed by the overflow of His grace.

Abraham didn't stop there. In fact, he haggled with the Almighty—"what about forty–five . . . or forty . . . or thirty . . . what about twenty?" . . . all the way down to ten. And for the sake of only ten the Lord still agreed to let the entire city live. But that was God's final offer (see 18:27–33).

Meanwhile, the two angels met Lot as soon as they arrived at the city of Sodom in the evening. He was sitting by the gate, apparently waiting to intercept them before they wandered into Sodom's evil haunts. When he saw the two, Lot bowed in respect for the Lord's personal emissaries and offered, "My lords, please come to my house for the night. There you can be refreshed to continue your journey in the morning." Initially refusing Lot's offer, they eventually agreed after his insistence. He must have persuaded them by insinuating that Sodom was not exactly hospitable to strangers (19:1–3).

Lot felt reasonably sure that his guests would be safe at his home. But before they retired for the night, men from all over the city, young and old, surrounded Lot's house shouting, "Where are the men who came to you tonight? Bring them out to us so that we can have sex with them" (19:5).

Mindful of his duties both as a host and a worshipper of Jehovah, Lot went out to reason with the frenzied mob. "My friends. Don't do this wicked thing," Lot pleaded. "I have two virgin daughters. Let me bring them out to you, and you can do what you like with them. But don't do anything to these men, for they have come under the protection of my home" (see 19:7–8). But they did not want the girls—they wanted the men.

"Get out of our way. . . . This fellow [Lot] came here as an alien, and now he wants to play the judge! We'll treat you worse than them" (19:9). When the mob rushed the house and threatened to beat down the door to take the two visitors and Lot by force, the angels pulled Lot back inside to safety and blinded the mob so they could not even find the door to the house. That was the final straw. Sodom and Gomorrah had passed the point of redemption.

The visitors then spoke:

> Do you have anyone else here [in Sodom]—sons–in–law,
> sons or daughters, or anyone else in the city who belongs
> to you? Get them out of here, because we are going to
> destroy this place. The outcry to the Lord against its peo-
> ple is so great that He has sent us to destroy it (19:12–13).

When first faced with bad news or danger, a common human reaction is denial. We refuse to think that it could happen to us. When Lot
found his sons–in–law, who were pledged to marry his daughters, and
warned them of the impending doom, they thought he was kidding.
They would not believe him.

As dawn approached, the angels urged Lot to flee with his family
or be killed when the city was obliterated. By the hand, they were led
out of the city and on their way to safety by the angels, for the Lord
had no desire to punish the good for the sins of the wicked. However,
for all of Abraham's negotiating with the Lord, He could not find even
ten righteous people in and around Sodom and Gomorrah.

The angels specified that Lot's family needed to "flee to the mountains"—and not look back (see 19:17). Why were they told not to look
back? It might have delayed their retreat to safety or caused them to be
angry with God for what He had done. But perhaps it would signify
that they valued their home, friends, and community more than their
relationship with God. As they fled, Lot's wife did look back—and was
changed to a pillar of salt (19:26). We will never know why she defied
explicit instructions. She may have resented Lot for bringing her to
Sodom in the first place, placing her and the girls in danger. Maybe she
was not as strong in her faith as Lot, for we have no information as to
her nationality or religious heritage. Whatever her reasons, she did not
survive the day, becoming instead part of the landscape of ruin.

Lot had said to the angels that it would be impossible to reach the
mountains in so little time, so the angels delayed the bombardment
until Lot and family arrived in the small town of Zoar nearby. Little did
the people of Zoar realize, Lot did them a great favor, for they would
have been toasted just like Sodom. By the time Lot and his two daughters reached the outskirts of Zoar, it was daybreak. As the sun rose,

super–heated sulphur rained down on Sodom and Gomorrah and the fertile plains around them, burning everything it touched (19:23–25).

Raining Fire

It is difficult to comprehend the scope of devastation that beset Sodom and Gomorrah. A certain amount of appreciation may be gained, however, if we compare what occurred to the eruption of Mount St. Helens in 1980. According to the *Encyclopedia Britannica,* this volcanic eruption blew out the north side of the mountain at 300 miles per hour, creating 230 square miles of destruction. With the temperature reaching 660°F and the power of twenty–four megatons of thermal energy, the blast of the eruption snapped 100–year–old trees, stripping them of their bark. The ash cloud grew to an altitude of approximately 80,000 feet, most of it falling back to earth within 300 miles of the blast site. Finer debris circled the earth for fifteen days. The entire 230–square–mile region instantly became a desolate wasteland unfit for habitation.

This description of the Mount St. Helens eruption would certainly fit the brief biblical account of the Lord's judgment on Sodom and Gomorrah—with one crucial exception: Nature's wrath brought sulfurous fire from beneath the earth; God's wrath brought it from above.

Early the next morning, Abraham went to a high place to survey the damage—the same place where he had met with the Lord. All he could see was smoke rising from where the cities had been (see 19:27–28). I wonder if Abraham had a twinge of regret, wondering if he could have done more to have prevented this from happening.

Lot's Daughters

The story of Lot and his family does not end here, for he became a single parent of two very headstrong, willful young women, who appear to have been every bit as pagan as the pagans they had lived among. We know little about them or their mother, but we do know how dysfunction breeds within a family when one spouse has strong spiritual beliefs and the other does not. To keep peace in the house, the stronger believer usually succumbs to a lower standard, weakening the overall spiritual health of the entire family. And just as commonly as genetic characteristics are passed down through generations, patterns of dysfunction also travel from parents to children to grandchildren—as the Bible illustrates the family lineage of dysfunction for ten generations. No one ever sins alone. Behaviors, addictions, and beliefs are bred from those closest to them or most influential in the generation before, and the results of those sins, in turn, are most deeply felt and repeated by those closest to us in the next.

Lot's daughters survived the fire and brimstone but created new family problems for generations to come. Their sinful natures never changed, although they had been saved from a fate reserved for sinners. When exposed to God's care, people either soften and become eager to accept His love, or they harden and retreat deeper into their sin—like the sun that either melts the ice or hardens the clay. The fate of Lot's daughters was the latter.

Lot and the remainder of his family quickly left Zoar and moved to the mountains, where they lived in a cave. It would have been difficult staying in Zoar. Once the word got out that he and his daughters were the sole survivors of the Sodom firestorm, Lot might have been marked for reprisal by the relatives of the recently charred (see 19:30). Living as refugees in their own homeland in a dark, smelly cave together would have been equally challenging. (I can imagine the angry words and glaring stares at home when the daughters remembered how Dad had offered them to the wild, sex–crazed mob.) These women were accustomed to a certain standard of living and must have missed it desperately. They had no desire to be "different"—either for God's sake or for their father's—and were willing to do whatever it took to return to the lives they knew before the destruction of Sodom.

"One day the older daughter said to the younger, 'Our father is old, and there is no man around here to lie with us, as is the custom all over the earth. Let's get our father to drink wine and then lie with him and preserve our family line through our father'" (19:31–32). So, that night the girls got Dad drunk, and the older daughter had sex with him while he slept, completely oblivious to what was happening. They repeated the action the next night with the younger sister, and they both became pregnant by their father, the unknowing accomplice (19:33–36).

What were Lot's thoughts when he learned that both of his girls were pregnant? Had he suffered so much grief with the loss of his wife and the city he once called home that he lacked the spiritual and emotional stamina to be the father the girls needed at that critical time?

The girls had their babies—both sons. The older daughter named hers Moab, who grew to become the father of the Moabites. The younger daughter named her son Ben–ammi, who became the father of the Ammonites (19:37–38). Throughout history, both tribes would be ancient, unforgiving enemies of Israel. If you thought the situation with Ishmael was bad, the one stemming from Moab and Ammon would be much worse.

Abimelech

Remember when Abraham and Sarah (when they were still Abram and Sarai) traveled to Egypt to avoid the famine in Canaan, and Abraham said that his wife was his sister for fear that Pharaoh would have him killed? Well—he did it again. And we thought that he had learned his lesson. This was not misrepresentation, spin, or just exaggeration—this was another flat–out lie.

Nearing the time of the promised baby to come, Abraham moved again to find pasture for his vast flocks. He traveled with his wife far from the still–smoldering remains of Sodom and Gomorrah toward the Negev, where he lived near the town of Kadesh—and briefly in Gerar. When the couple and their entourage first arrived in Gerar, Abraham introduced Sarah as his sister (see 20:1–2). It seems that our boy Abraham, for all his faith and courage, still had a difficult time telling the truth in this one particular area of his life.

Hearing she was available, King Abimelech of Gerar sent for Sarah and took her to live in the palace. If this story is placed in some type of chronological sequence, then we know that Sarah was waiting for the birth of Isaac, making her at least ninety years old. She must have been one well–preserved woman to be so desirable. Maybe they lived better in those days.

One night, as King Abimelech was sleeping, the Lord came to him in a dream and said, "You are as good as dead because of the woman you have taken; she is a married woman" (20:3). This was not just a dream but a vision from God—a vision that did not have a happy ending. Abimelech was going to die, and he had only just settled Sarah into the harem quarters with the other wives to see how she would fit in!

Panic–stricken, Abimelech asked, "Lord, will you destroy an inno-cent nation? Did he [Abraham] not say to me, 'She is my sister,' and didn't she [Sarah] also say, 'He is my brother'? I have done this with a clear conscience and clean hands" (20:4–5).

The Lord spoke to Abimelech again in the dream: "Yes, I know you did this with a clear conscience, and so I have kept you from sinning against Me. That is why I did not let you touch her. Now return the man's wife, for he is a prophet, and he will pray for you and you will live. But if you do not return her, you may be sure that you and all yours will die" (20:6–7). God clearly made Abimelech an offer he couldn't refuse, for it says that early the next morning (probably well before sunrise) Abimelech summoned his cabinet and reiterated his late–night discussion with the Almighty.

The king's advisors could handle almost any national emergency—but not a direct confrontation with God. Already briefed on what had happened at Sodom and Gomorrah, they had no intention of being "brimstone–nuked" the same way. Once the hastily convened council broke up, Abimelech immediately called Abraham in and questioned him. "What have you done to us? How have I wronged you that you have brought such great guilt upon me and my kingdom? You have done things to me that should not be done. . . . What was your reason for doing this?" (20:9–10).

In his explanation, Abraham had assumed, first of all, that Abimelech was not a God–fearing man. This apparently was a wrong assumption to make. Then he proceeded to justify his definition of "sister" by describing Sarah as "the daughter of my Father," though she, of course, had a different mother (see 20:11–12).

Eager to make amends with God, Abimelech presented Abraham with sheep, cattle, slaves, and servants as he brought Sarah back from the palace, safe and unharmed. Abimelech also told Abraham, "My land is before you; live wherever you like," opening opportunities to travel and settle without interference. And to Sarah, "I am giving your brother 1,000 shekels of silver. This is to cover the offense against you before all who are with you; you are completely vindicated" (20:14-16). Not a bad deal—Sarah was able to reside briefly at the palace, being preened and pampered, and the family fortune was amended considerably. When the Lord set out to bless Abraham and Sarah, He didn't do it halfway.

Abimelech was relieved to have the Abraham/Sarah issue resolved for a much more personal reason—one that threatened his kingdom as much as being struck dead. While Sarah was in the palace, all the women of the king's entire household were on a divinely mandated birth control program so that none could conceive. When Abraham prayed, the Lord restored fertility to the kingdom and restored it so well, in fact, that Sarah became pregnant just as the Lord had promised.

Finally, Sarah gave birth to a son, and Abraham named him Isaac, the son of laughter. When the lad was eight days old he was circumcised as commanded—a reminder of the covenant between God and His people (21:4). Sarah remarked, "God has brought me laughter, and everyone who hears about this will laugh with me. . . . Who would have said to Abraham that Sarah would nurse children? Yet I have borne him a son in his old age" (21:6–7). Responding with laughter may have been a reasonable first reaction under the circumstances, but parenting would prove to be a far more challenging task than Abraham and Sarah ever imagined.

Chapter 9

Isaac

"You're Abraham's Boy"

Nothing is written about Isaac's childhood—what he did or what he looked like. We have no idea if he resembled Mom or Dad or even Grandpa Terah. But from what little information we have, we can try to piece together an impression of Isaac's personality and how his family functioned—or didn't. We do know that Isaac was the favored child of elderly, probably doting parents and, as such, would have been wealthier than most of his peers. He could have been the "little prince" of the tribe—heir to Abraham's extensive holdings, possibly making him a bit of a brat. Having Isaac as her first so late in life, Sarah might never have relaxed and allowed Isaac to sustain the little dings and injuries that come with being a kid without going into a panic.

Technically, Isaac was not Abraham's firstborn son—that was Ishmael. But their ages were far enough apart that each son might have been treated as a first and only child. Isaac, however, probably had a special relationship with his dad, who was certainly older and wiser than the fathers of Isaac's friends. Isaac undoubtedly grew to be a confident child, protected by a strong, loving father.

By this time Ishmael, Isaac's half brother, was a teenager. And, like teenagers of every generation, he was ready to test the boundaries of parental control. Although we cannot be sure if Ishmael was disrespectful, we do know that divided loyalties and simmering hostilities existed in the household. Scripture picks up the story with Isaac as an infant or early toddler: "The child grew and was weaned, and on the day Isaac was weaned Abraham held a great feast" (21:8). Did Abraham have a feast for Ishmael, too? Did the old man mark the birth of that son with a similar celebration? I doubt it, given the history of hostility between Sarah and Hagar—both fighting for Abraham's affections and jousting for their child's status as "favored son."

Favoritism, wherein one sibling receives better treatment or more attention at the other's expense, is a hallmark of dysfunctional families. Isaac was loved more, and everyone knew it—especially Hagar and Ishmael. Sarah saw that Ishmael was "mocking" (a trait he picked up from his mother Hagar, no doubt) and demanded that Abraham send him away—along with his mother. So filled with fury, she could not even bear to say Hagar's name aloud (see 21:10). Sarah's hatred for Hagar and her offspring had festered from those early days of feeling inadequate as a wife who bore no children, and that lingering hurt poisoned her ability to embrace that side of the family.

"The matter distressed Abraham greatly because it concerned his son" (21:11). Abraham probably could have been impartial in dealing with any other child or set of parents, but not regarding anything that involved his son. He had to keep peace with his wife, yet he needed to maintain a sense of harmony in the everyday activities of the tribe he was leading. He could not keep order, however, with undercurrents of mockery flowing from Ishmael and Hagar.

Abraham may have tried what he had done the last time Sarah had given an ultimatum about Hagar—that is, make no decision and hope things would eventually right themselves. Unfortunately, serious family conflicts rarely correct themselves or improve over time. Instead, time serves only to solidify the grudge and intensify the hurt. In the relationship between Cain and Abel, time allowed the anger to grow, resulting in murder, not reconciliation. The potential for history to repeat itself was gaining strength in Abraham's household.

I imagine Abraham spent long nights praying quietly in the dark while the rest of the family slept, begging God for a solution to this seemingly unsolvable problem. God assured Abraham that both boys would have a special destiny—Isaac would extend the covenant and Ishmael would be a patriarch in his own right (21:12–13). Sounds simple enough. Realizing that both rival factions could not live so close to each other, Abraham gave Hagar and Ishmael a supply of food and a skin of water and sent them away to start a new life.

But rather than head toward civilization, Hagar and Ishmael may have gotten lost because she wandered into the Desert of Beersheba (see 21:14). When the water ran out and it appeared certain that they were going to die, Hagar placed Ishmael under a bush, perhaps in the only shade to be found. She could not bear to hear him moan and cry, so she moved away a few yards to pray and wait for death to end it all. But God sent an angel to help, and the angel of God called to Hagar, "What is the matter, Hagar? Do not be afraid; God has heard the boy crying as he lies there. Lift the boy up and take him by the hand, for I will make him into a great nation" (21:17–18). The heavenly messenger then showed her a well of water close by. The Lord kept His promise and continued to watch over Ishmael.

Since the history of Israel unfolds through Abraham, Isaac, and their descendants, we know little more about Ishmael. The boy and his mom survived to live in the Desert of Paran, where he became a proficient archer. When he was old enough, Hagar found a woman from Egypt to be his wife (see 21:19–21). From these few facts, we can determine the following: 1. As an archer Ishmael learned to be a capable, if not formidable, warrior; 2. Living in the desert made him hard, self–reliant and perhaps embittered, thinking Isaac received the better promise; and 3. An Egyptian wife would unite two nationalities against a common enemy one day.

Beersheba

Abraham went on with his life, building up his holdings and increasing his prestige by making profitable deals for grazing and water rights. At one point, Abraham's people had a dispute over a well with the citizens of Gerar—subjects of King Abimelech. Remember him— the one who almost married Sarah? Abimelech's servants "allegedly" had seized a well dug by Abraham's workers. We do not know who started the fight, but we do know that Abimelech and Phicol, the commander of the king's forces, negotiated admirably with Abraham, resulting in a mutually beneficial arrangement. Abimelech, fully aware of the special protection Abraham enjoyed, first wanted to establish an understanding: "God is with you in everything you do. Now swear to me here before God that you will not deal falsely with me or my children or my descendants. Show to me and the country where you are living as an alien the same kindness I have shown to you" (21:22–23). Abraham agreed, enabling the men to bargain in good faith and avoiding any escalating hostilities. Abraham then outlined his grievances, expressing his concerns for his people and flocks if they were to be deprived of ready access to water.

The king, obviously taken aback by this news and not just playing dumb, replied, "I don't know who has done this. You did not tell me, and I heard about it only today" (21:26). We would think that the king would have been better informed. Trusting the king's good faith, Abraham brought a gift of sheep and cattle to Abimelech. Aside from these gifts, Abraham separated several ewe lambs from the rest as an extra gift to the king, since some residual doubt still lingered as to the ownership of the well. The two men made a treaty, mutually swearing to respect property and human rights. They called the treaty site *Beersheba*, meaning "well of the oath." In a portion of land that belonged to the Philistines, Abraham planted a tamarisk tree as a reminder of the treaty (see 21:27–33).

The Philistines (descendants of Abimelech) and the Hebrews would share a long and notable history of warfare for generations to come. The famed incident of David and the Philistine champion Goliath would be one of a prolonged series of clashes. But for the moment, there was peace as Abraham lived in relative harmony with his Philistine neighbors and with his own family—a long–lasting peace that Abraham was not accustomed to in his life.

"You are going to do WHAT to our son?"

About the only thing in life that remains constant is change. Abraham's family enjoyed a long period of peace and security, but "some time later God tested Abraham" (22:1). How much later? We can only presume that Abraham and Isaac had been allowed some years of quality time together before their test of trust and obedience was given.

God said, "Take your son, your only son, Isaac, whom you love, and go to the region of Moriah. Sacrifice him there as a burnt offering on one of the mountains I will tell you about" (22:2). Abraham's faith was being put to the ultimate test. He had to follow the Lord's lead, purely on faith, when every part of him screamed to disobey. What would our reaction have been to such a request? *Take my child, the one promised to us as a gift in our old age, and You want me to do what? Offer him as a sacrifice—to show what? My devotion, my commitment? Can't there be some better way to accomplish this without killing my son?* Perhaps Abraham had wondered if he could trade places with Isaac—and be the sacrifice, instead—since most fathers would do almost anything to protect their children from harm.

How do you suppose Abraham shared this news with Sarah?

"Hi, honey. How was your day? Hey, I was just talking to the Lord. He says, 'Hi,' by the way. Well, guess what? He wants me to take Isaac on a field trip."

"That's nice, dear. Where to?"

"He wants us to go out toward Mount Moriah. Great view, plenty of things for Isaac to see and do."

"Like what, Abraham?"

"Well, you wouldn't really be interested. It gets a little technical."

"Try me, Abe. And tell me what's going on. Why do I get the feeling you're hiding something from me?"

"Here it is. I am supposed to take Isaac and offer him as a sacrifice to the Lord."

Just about that time I imagine Abraham had to duck to avoid a frying pan hurled at his head. At the very least, plenty of tears were shed that night. But Abraham and Sarah were also in agreement that the Lord had never failed to protect and sustain them, and God could be trusted to do so again.

If there was any anguish or tossing and turning, it did not affect Abraham's actions, for "early the next morning Abraham got up and saddled his donkey. He took with him two of his servants and his son Isaac. When he had cut enough wood for the burnt offering, he set out for the place God had told him about" (22:3). After three days on the road, Abraham found the place where the offering was to be made. He said to his servants, "Stay here with the donkey while I and the boy go over there. We will worship and then we will come back to you" (24:5). By the comment "we will come back," not "I will come back," we can surmise that Abraham must have felt that God would spare Isaac's life.

Isaac hauled the wood for the offering as they proceeded to their appointed spot. As they walked, Isaac was the first to break the silence and ask, "The fire and wood are here, . . . but where is the lamb for the burnt offering?" (22:7). The kid wasn't stupid. He knew there was supposed to be a perfect animal for the offering, and they had not brought one. But as long as he was with his dad, everything would be all right.

Abraham probably strained to reply so as not to sound afraid for the boy's safety, "God Himself will provide the lamb for the burnt offering, my son" (22:8). Abraham built an altar from stones, then he tied Isaac and laid him on the altar atop the wood. I wonder if there was any struggle? Scripture does not mention resistance on Isaac's part. Perhaps Isaac, for all his later faults, inherited one great character trait from Abraham—faith. He believed that Abraham and God knew what was best, and he could trust them both with his life, and his death.

Abraham took the knife and prepared to kill his son. In the face of horrid fear, sadness, and pain, Abraham was willing to do the unthinkable—because the Lord required it. Just before the fatal plunge of the blade, the Lord spoke. "Abraham! . . . Do not lay a hand on the boy. . . . Do not do anything to him. Now I know that you fear God, because you have not withheld from Me your son, your only son" (22:11–12).

God had no intention of allowing Abraham to commit murder just to make a point. Given the failure of mankind at Sodom and Gomorrah and of Lot and his children, and even the weakness of Abraham, who sometimes had a difficult time telling the truth, God needed to confirm Abraham as a man of faith and worthy father of nations. Although the Lord knew what would happen, He needed Abraham to learn the lesson for himself. As soon as the Lord stayed the execution, Abraham looked and saw a ram caught by its horns in the bushes. A true sacrificial animal was provided, just as Abraham had promised Isaac. The Lord was pleased, and He honored Abraham for his willingness to sacrifice his son as an offering of obedience and trust (see 22:13,15–18).

Abraham and Isaac returned to the waiting servants, and they all set off for Beersheba—where Ishmael lived. There is no indication of a feast after Isaac was spared. (Personally, I would have thrown the biggest survivor party anyone had ever seen.) Scripture states that "Abraham stayed in Beersheba" (22:19), but it does not mention Sarah being with him. Was there a rift in the relationship that was left unmended? Before leaving for Moriah with the resolve to sacrifice Isaac, did Abraham face another ultimatum from Sarah—words to the effect of "If you leave, don't bother coming back"?

After some time in Beersheba, Abraham received an update on other family members that he had not seen for awhile. Milcah, his sister–in–law, had eight sons. One of them, Bethuel, had a daughter Rebekah (see 22:20–23). Then abruptly the story shifts to the death of Sarah, who lived to be 127 years old. Scripture says, "She died at Kiriath Arba (that is, Hebron) in the land of Canaan, and Abraham went to mourn for Sarah and to weep over her" (23:2). Maybe Abraham wished he could have done or said something to make things right with Sarah before she died. All he could do was mourn and afford Sarah in death the love he had felt for her in life.

Abraham asked the Hittites, in whose land he was mourning his wife, if he could buy some of their property to bury her. The Hittites replied, "You are a mighty prince among us. Bury your dead in the choicest of our tombs. None of us will refuse you his tomb for burying your dead" (23:6). They knew not to antagonize such a great man. Better to have him owe you a favor and make him a friend than to initiate a grievance and make him an enemy. Abraham thanked them for their kind offer, but he wanted to buy the cave of Machpelah from Ephron, son of Zohar, and was willing to pay full price so that no one could ever lay claim to it (see 23:8–9). We all need places held in community to mark the passing of time and family history. Abraham was no different. He and Ephron agreed on a price of 400 shekels of silver, and the deal was done. Abraham buried Sarah in the cave, which stood in a field at Machpelah. This became the first piece of real estate Abraham and his family could call their own (see 23:16–20), and it marked the first installment of the Lord's prophecy and promise.

Chapter 10

Rebekah

Finding Isaac a Wife

We don't read too much about Isaac during his young manhood, as we do with many other Bible characters. In fact, of the three commonly invoked names of Israel's patriarchs, Isaac gets the least coverage. We never hear of his adventures defending the family, driving out marauding kings, interceding with God for cities, or doing anything really noteworthy other than being the father of Jacob and Esau—and not doing a very good job at it either. Had the sacrifice experience changed him? Did Isaac fear that one day God would ask for a sacrifice again and not provide a ram?

Now that his family had a cemetery plot to call their own, Abraham, who was "well advanced in years," wanted to find a wife for Isaac to perpetuate the line. It was also crucial that Isaac's spouse be a relative so that the family's inheritance would not make further detours than it already had—with Ishmael and with Lot's grandchildren. Abraham also had a bone of contention with Canaanite women, who were both unrelated and outside the covenant relationship with God. You may ask why Isaac could not be trusted with the adult responsibility of finding a wife on his own. He was the child of promise, you see. Abraham needed to be sure that his son found "a good girl"—one with similar traditions, values, and religious heritage. So Abraham decided to appoint his chief steward for the task and made him promise not to select a local woman from Canaan to be Isaac's wife. Instead, he would have to travel back to Abraham's homeland to find a bride from among the relatives (see 24:2–4). The steward asked, "What if the woman is unwilling to come back with me to this land? Shall I then take your son back to the country you came from?" (24:5).

Abraham was adamant. "Make sure that you do not take my son back there. . . . The Lord . . . will send His angel before you so that you can get a wife for my son from there. If the woman is unwilling to come back with you, then you will be released from this oath of mine. Only do not take my son back there" (24:6–8).

The steward took ten camels and loaded them with the essentials along with gold, silver, jewelry, fine embroidered fabric, clothing spun from their finest wool, butter–soft tanned lambskin jackets and other goodies that might entice a father to allow his daughter to marry Isaac. The caravan set out for Aram Naharaim (northwest Mesopotamia) to locate Abraham's brother, Nahor. If a wife for Isaac could not be found there, at least Nahor could set the search in the right direction (see 24:10). Arriving outside the town of Nahor in early evening, the steward tied up the camels by the well just before the women came to draw water. He prayed:

> O Lord, God of my master Abraham, give me success today, and show kindness to my master. . . . May it be that when I say to a girl, "Please let down your jar that I may have a drink," and she says, "Drink, and I'll water your camels too"—let her be the one You have chosen for Your servant Isaac. (24:12–14)

If a woman volunteered to do more than was normally expected, the steward would know he had found someone with a willing heart, positive attitude, and sensational work ethic.

Before the steward could remove his prayer shawl, he looked and there was Rebekah, Abraham's distant grandniece, coming to the well. She was the very girl he had hoped to find, but he did not know it yet. Rebekah was a knockout, and he wondered if she might be an excellent mate for Isaac. As she headed back to town after filling her water jar, the steward hurried over to say, "Please give me a little water from your jar" (see 24:15–17). Without the slightest bit of hesitation she lowered the container and gave him a drink.

After the steward drank his fill, Rebekah said the exact words he wanted to hear: "I'll draw water for your camels too, until they have finished drinking" (24:19). So she quickly emptied her jar into the trough, ran back to the well to draw more water, and drew enough for all his camels (24:20). The significance of this last statement can be easily overlooked. Camels are known for their ability to go long periods without water, but once they are thirsty, a single camel can drink up to 53 gallons (200 liters) of water at one sitting. A standard oil barrel holds 55 gallons, so you can begin to visualize the amount of water Rebekah offered to draw for these camels—all ten of them! Five hundred–thirty gallons of water, drawn one jar at a time from a well and then *schlepped* to the trough, is a massive commitment of time and effort, which Rebekah willingly made to strangers. It might have taken her all night to accomplish.

"Without saying a word, the man watched her closely to learn whether or not the Lord had made his journey successful" (24:21). I am a little dismayed that he didn't offer to help, but that would have been considered an insult with potentially serious repercussions. He must have thought, *This one's a keeper!* In a modern scenario, Rebekah might have met this stranger, bought him a cup of coffee, then offered to fill his car with gas, change the oil, and wash and wax it by hand.

When the camels finished drinking, the man gave Rebekah a gold nose ring and two gold bracelets. Nose rings, customarily worn in the left nostril, were high fashion in the Middle East in those days. Since these gifts were offered to her, not to her father as part of a matrimonial bargaining process, they were simply given in appreciation for her kindness. The steward asked, "Whose daughter are you? Please tell me, is there room in your father's house for us to spend the night?" (24:23). He was impressed and did not want this lovely woman to get away without making some serious inquiries.

Rebekah finally introduced herself. "I am the daughter of Bethuel, the son that Milcah bore to Nahor," adding almost as an afterthought, "We have plenty of straw and fodder [for the camels], as well as room for you to spend the night" (24:24–25). The steward gratefully prayed, thanking the Lord for blessing this matrimonial mission and leading him to the house of his master's relatives (see 24:26–27). (My impression is that when Rebekah headed home to show everyone the treasures she had received, the steward jumped up from his place of prayer and began a little football end–zone celebration dance.) Rebekah ran to tell the family all that had transpired at the well. As soon as her brother Laban heard the news, he ran back even faster, not wanting to lose the man with the camels and the fancy gold jewelry. Laban welcomed the steward and his men as honored guests.

After everyone arrived at the house and the camels were cared for, the men cleaned up for dinner. But the steward could not eat until he explained the true reason for his trip. Bursting at the seams with excitement, he told the entire story, leaving out no detail and emphasizing God's involvement throughout (see 24:34–47). He concluded by saying,

> I praised the Lord, the God of my master Abraham, who had led me on the right road to get the granddaughter of my master's brother for his son. Now if you will show kindness and faithfulness to my master, tell me; and if not, tell me, so I may know which way to turn (24: 48–49).

This was a marriage proposal wrapped in the Lord's blessing. Simply stated, would Rebekah be allowed to return with them to marry Isaac?

Laban and Bethuel considered the proposal for a moment and decided, "This is from the Lord; we can say nothing to you one way or the other. Here is Rebekah; take her and go, and let her become the wife of your master's son, as the Lord has directed" (24:50–51). When the steward heard that his quest was over, he gave thanks to God and then lavished expensive gifts on Rebekah's mother and brother. Abraham's emissaries finished dinner, assured that they would be returning home with a bride. When they awoke the next morning, the men were eager to be on their way. But Laban and Rebekah's mother hesitated, asking for a ten–day extension before Rebekah could leave. Immediately alarm bells must have gone off in the steward's head as he sensed a stalling tactic. Did Laban want more money? "Quit fooling around," the steward demanded. "Do we have a deal or not? I have to get back to my master with the good news as soon as possible" (see 24:55–56).

Realizing that no one had ever asked Rebekah how she felt about the offer, the mother and brother then said, "Let's call the girl and ask her about it" (24:57). It makes you wonder about their motivation since the family referred to Rebekah as "the girl," as if she were some kind of commodity to be traded. "Will you go with this man?" they asked her.

Rebekah replied without hesitation, "I will go." So off she went with Abraham's men and her nurse—toward the groom–to–be, Isaac. She was on the road to meet the man with whom she would spend the rest of her life, a man unknown to her until the day before—and without even a picture to go on. (King Henry VIII of England had already had one marriage annulled, two wives executed, and one dead from natural causes, and was looking for someone attractive without a political agenda. That person was Anne of Cleves. Unfortunately all that Henry had was a portrait of her and the testimony of people who vouched for her beauty. When they actually met, the king realized that both the portrait and the testimonials were pure fiction. That marriage was dissolved almost before the ink dried on the certificate.)

Regardless of her apprehension, though, Rebekah went willingly. Maybe it was the idea of love, the prospect of adventure, the eagerness to start her own family, or a willingness to respond to the hand of God on her life that gave her strength to leave.

The scene changes to a field out in the Negev, near the town of Beer Lahai Roi. Isaac had been meditating one evening when he looked up and saw camels approaching. About the same time, Rebekah looked out from her camel and saw Isaac coming toward them. Getting down, she asked the steward, "Who is that man in the field coming to meet us?" When he told her that the man approaching was his master, Isaac, she "took her veil and covered herself" (see 24:65). Although Rebekah had not worn the veil in front of the servants or anyone else, she immediately began her life with Isaac with propriety and according to all the traditions of their ancestors.

Whether Isaac was briefed before or after Abraham, Dad was still the one in charge and would be until he died. Although Isaac may have been instantly smitten by Rebekah as they first met under the stars in that field, it was Abraham who would make the final decision for Isaac to marry or not. But eventually Isaac brought Rebekah to his mother's tent, now his own, as a young man taking a wife, and he married her. "So she became his wife, and he loved her; and Isaac was comforted after his mother's death" (24:67).

Isaac remained under his father's controlling influence for another thirty–five years, for in their culture, no child—not even the eldest son—became fully independent until dad was dead and gone. Can you imagine Isaac being viewed as "daddy's little boy" as long as Abraham was still alive? "Young man, I don't care how old you are," Abraham might have said. "As long as you are living in my camp, under my tent, you will obey my rules—or you and Rebekah are grounded."

Soon, though, Isaac would take on a greater leadership role as patriarch. Would he be adequate for the task? How decisive a leader would Isaac become, having lived in the shadow of his strong–willed parents? Given the fact that Rebekah was a "comfort" who replaced a special relationship Isaac shared with Sarah, Isaac could be described as a "mama's boy"—not strong like Abraham or handy like Noah or deeply spiritual like Enoch. Instead, he would live the rest of his life in the shadow of his more famous offspring, Jacob and Esau, trying to father them—and not doing a very good job at it.

The Torch Is Passed

After a suitable period of mourning, Abraham remarried. Sarah, the love of his youth, could never be replaced. So it was not that Abraham loved his next wife Keturah more or less, but differently. Abraham and Sarah had been through the move to Canaan, the separation from Lot, the destruction of Sodom and Gomorrah, and the miraculous birth of Isaac in their old age. Scripture says that Keturah bore him six sons who went on to have notable families of their own (see 25:1–4). Chances are, Abraham was not as involved in their lives as he had been with Isaac. But then, he was never commanded to offer any of them as a sacrifice. The sacrifice experience had changed Abraham, though, for he never had a problem telling the truth again.

Before he died, Abraham left everything he owned to Isaac. But while Abraham was still able to direct his own affairs, he gave gifts to his concubines and other children before he sent them away—much like changing the staff at the White House when a new President is elected. Things would be hard enough for Isaac, taking over as the keeper of God's covenant, without having so many reminders of the old administration living nearby (see 25:5–6). Abraham was 175 when he died at the end of a long and productive life, "an old man and full of years" (see 25:7–8). Isaac and Ishmael put aside their differences long enough to bury their father in the same cave in Machpelah where Sarah had been buried years before. Following the funeral, Ishmael and Isaac parted ways. Then as now, families apparently reunited at weddings and funerals, only to return to their own lives immediately after—until the next landmark event.

Isaac proceeded to fulfill his destiny, as Scripture states. Ishmael is never mentioned at length in the Bible again, for he was not a central character in completing God's covenant with the fledgling nation of Israel. What is mentioned are the twelve descendants of Ishmael, who became tribal rulers of Ishmael's family—just as twelve sons would form the basis of Jacob's family (see 25:12–16). Neither Isaac's nor Ishmael's descendants learned much from the failures and decisions of their combined history, and as such, were doomed to repeat them. As each generation grew farther apart, more and more injustices and injuries of the past were repeated. The Bible says Ishmael lived to be 137, and his descendants "lived in hostility toward all their brothers" (25:18). As the years increased, so did this venom of hatred in the bloodline of our dysfunctional family. What a legacy; what a shame.

Chapter 11

Jacob and Esau

The Feuding Brothers

During Abraham's last years, Isaac was still childless as he hovered on the brink of becoming the next family patriarch. He knew he needed an heir in order to avoid the same problem his parents had with Hagar and Ishmael. And for once, the dysfunctional family did something right—"Isaac prayed to the Lord on behalf of his wife, because she was barren" (25:21). He remembered to seek the Lord before stumbling into trouble, not after he had already made a mess of things. And God abundantly answered his request for a child. Rebekah became pregnant—with twins. As the babies grew, they jostled inside her as if playing football, making things extraordinarily uncomfortable (see 25:22).

God explained to Rebekah, "Two nations are in your womb, and two peoples from within you will be separated; one people will be stronger than the other, and the older will serve the younger" (25:23). As if having twins wasn't complicated enough! Inside Rebekah were the makings of a bitter rivalry—one child to be honored, the other to be his brother's servant. The elder being subject to the younger would conflict with the custom of the firstborn child laying claim to the inheritance. From the start, Isaac and Rebekah would have a difficult time raising their twins. The stage was set for them to be preferential, giving rise to unfair comparisons and unhealthy competition—a prime recipe for conflict, envy, and dysfunction.

Isaac was sixty when Rebekah gave birth, and the twin boys could not have been more different. The firstborn had a ruddy complexion and lots of red hair, and he was called Esau, meaning "red." The second child came a moment later, grasping the back of his brother's foot. Isaac and Rebekah named their second son Jacob, meaning the "grasper" or "supplanter," which was fitting since he would displace his older sibling (see 25: 25–26). Although separated at birth by mere seconds, the relationship between these brothers was distant and strained from the beginning, and it only got worse.

Esau became a skillful hunter and capable outdoorsman, providing extra meat for the family table—a handy son to have around. Brother Jacob, on the other hand, "was a quiet man, staying among the tents" (25:27). One brother liked to be outside getting dirty, while the other liked the "great indoors," cooking and participating in more refined pursuits. Neither was a better man than the other, of course; they were just different. Both boys should have been allowed to develop their own personalities while being equally valued by their parents. That was not the case, however.

Isaac, who liked the taste of fresh game, loved his son Esau more, while Rebekah preferred Jacob, who stayed at home and was "mom's little helper." No doubt, both parents took sides whenever sibling rivalries erupted, but playing favorites is not the way to raise children. Worse than Isaac and Rebekah's habit of taking sides was their conditional love for their sons, based not on who the boys were but on what they could do. Consequently, rather than being best friends and playmates, Jacob and Esau were perpetual rivals, knowing that they were constantly being evaluated on their actions.

In most families, siblings notoriously fight one another. But when an outside party enters the equation, siblings are also famous for defending the brother or sister who may have been scum just moments before. Nowhere in Scripture does it indicate that Jacob or Esau ever defended the other. Since Isaac and Rebekah were the ones feeding this sibling hatred with their comparisons, is it any wonder the boys did not aspire to proper family values?

Lentils for a Birthright

One day Jacob was preparing lentil stew when Esau came in from hunting, hungry enough to eat anything in sight—a typical teenage appetite.

"Jakey," Esau asked. "How about sharing a little bit of that stew? I don't know what's in it, little brother, but it smells good. I'm so hungry I could eat a camel."

Normally Jacob's reaction may have been to whine or run away and complain to Mama. But this time Jacob had something in mind. "Sure, I can do that. First sell me your birthright. It's a fair trade. I'll give you all the stew you can eat; you give me your birthright" (see 25:31). The birthright involved the special inheritance rights and privileges reserved for the firstborn child. It also entailed the heir's position in the transference of tribal authority and leadership. For someone as wealthy as Isaac, that could amount to some serious money for the lucky son who held the birthright in his investment portfolio. Although recognized as legal and binding, these rights could be transferred.

Esau replied with an exaggeration common to young people who think they are starving when in fact they are only slightly hungry: "Look, I am about to die. . . . What good is the birthright to me?" (25:32). Jacob made Esau swear to the transaction, no doubt having it signed, witnessed, and notarized. The transfer was irreversible.

Jacob may have unfairly played on Esau's vulnerable state of extreme hunger, but Esau had treated something sacred and not to be squandered as having no value. In a family intent on breeding unhealthy feelings of self–doubt perpetrated by constant comparisons, Esau's reaction as a young adult was, finally, not to care—about family, God, inheritance, or his future. Esau ate his fill, but his birthright was gone forever. Jacob returned to his cooking with a self–satisfied smirk, knowing that he, the little brother, had won big–time! He had won, yes, but not without great cost.

Abimelech and the Next Generation

Soon the whole family became hungry when another famine struck the region. As patriarch, Isaac was responsible for the safety of his whole tribe. Needing to make arrangements to feed everyone, his first thought was to travel to Egypt by way of Gerar. So he paid a visit to Abimelech, king of the Philistines, who lived in Gerar. (This particular Abimelech may have been a descendant of the Abimelech that tried to add Sarah to his harem. Unlike kings of England, the Philistines did not add Roman numerals to their names—possibly because there were no Romans to make numerals yet.) While still in Gerar, the Lord told Isaac to stay where he was—God would guarantee enough food for all. Isaac listened to God and stayed in Gerar (see 26:1–6).

No sooner had Isaac and Rebekah set up their tents, than Isaac was asked about his relationship with Rebekah. (She must have been quite a looker even in her sixties and after having twins!) You know how certain behaviors seem to perpetuate from generation to generation? Well, the one that carried over in this family was the habit of passing wives off as sisters. Isaac, afraid to claim Rebekah as his wife, reacted in a panic by saying, "She is my sister." (Here we go again.)

After the couple had been in Gerar "a long time," Abimelech looked out his window one day and saw Isaac and Rebekah caressing with a passion reserved for husbands and wives—not brothers and sisters (26:8). "Whoa, Jack! That's no sister. That's his wife!" exclaimed the king. Then he promptly summoned Isaac to the palace and said, "She is really your wife! Why did you say, 'She is my sister'? . . . What is this you have done to us? One of the men might well have slept with your wife, and you would have brought guilt upon us" (26:9–10).

Isaac gave the standard response: "Because I thought I might lose my life." This reply always seemed reasonable enough to the kings of Gerar to end their protests. Abimelech ordered anyone who tried to molest Rebekah (or Isaac, for that matter) to be put to death on the spot (see 26:11). Isaac and his whole family had the protection of the king, as did Abraham before him.

The whole tribe stayed around Gerar and planted crops, and in spite of the famine, the Lord blessed them with a huge harvest that first year. Isaac became increasingly wealthy over time, and the Philistines grew envious of his good fortune and either wanted to slow him down or "get a piece of the action." In a country where rain was such an irregular occurrence, control of the local wells and water supply was the surest way to drive out unwanted competition. So the Philistines filled in all the wells that had been dug during Abraham's time (when the first Abimelech offered free range of the land without interference). Then the current king said to Isaac, "Move away . . . you have become too powerful for us" (26:16). Rather than fight a war over water rights, Isaac and company moved—but not far—into the Valley of Gerar and settled there.

Isaac's men re–opened wells that had been filled by the Philistines, and got right back to business. But whenever the Philistine shepherds discovered the wells, they immediately contested the Hebrews' rights, claiming the wells as their own. This quarreling over ownership of well sites continued until finally the Hebrews dug a new well where no one disputed their claim, and Isaac named it *Rehoboth*, meaning "room," saying, "Now the Lord has given us room and we will flourish in the land" (26:22). Abimelech later came to see Isaac near Beersheba, accompanied by his personal advisor and the commander of his forces.

Realizing that God's hand of protection was on everything that Isaac did, the king proposed a treaty: "There ought to be a sworn agreement between us. . . . Let us make a treaty with you that you will do us no harm, just as we . . . treated you well and sent you away in peace" (26:28–29). The two leaders then celebrated their newly forged friendship with a grand feast, and the next day they swore an oath to each other. For that moment, Isaac showed a flash of leadership skills that would have made his father proud, for he had negotiated water rights and a peace treaty while giving away nothing. If only Isaac could have exhibited the same brilliance and wisdom when it came to running his own household.

Esau's Rebellion

One of the prime concerns that all parents have for their children is finding a good mate. Things were no different with Isaac and Rebekah. In most cases, marriages work best where commonality exists between husband and wife as well as between families. That is not to say that marriages that cut across ethnic and racial lines don't work, for they do. Commonality only decreases the potential for adjustment problems with each other and the in–laws. Esau, however, did not care what his folks thought. Having heard the prophecy that the "older will serve the younger" all his life, he had no hesitation about driving his parents crazy as it related to his choice of spouse. In fact, we could assume that he rather enjoyed creating turmoil and controversy.

When Esau was forty years old, he married not once but twice—to Judith and Basemath, who were both Hittites (see 26:34). All the Bible says about Isaac and Rebekah's reaction is that the daughters–in–law "were a source of grief" (26:35) to them. We are never told what that grief implied, but we can imagine the constant tension in the camp. The girls were not bad people, but their type of worship, so contrary to that of Isaac's family, involved idols, bizarre sexual practices, and ritual prostitution.

Blame, however, should be spread among all the members of Isaac's family—not just directed at Esau and his defiant behavior. All that grief and tension that existed within the family was the outcome of many years of dysfunctional parenting. Isaac and Rebekah could have taken Esau's side, for example, in the matter of the birthright. They could have done many things as the boys were growing up, but they did not. So any parental heartache Isaac and Rebekah experienced was of their own doing. Often, grief is of our own making.

Lies, Deception, and Rage

As Isaac aged, his eyesight and general health deteriorated. He knew the time had come to pass along the family blessing to make for a smooth transition upon his demise. Isaac called for Esau, his personal favorite, and said to his firstborn:

> I am now an old man and don't know the day of my death. Now then, get your weapons—your quiver and bow— and go out to the open country to hunt some wild game for me. Prepare me the kind of tasty food I like and bring it to me to eat, so that I may give you my blessing before I die (27:2–4).

It seems a shame that Isaac could not do the right thing without first making conditions. Why could he not say, "My son, I am old and may not have much time. I want you to know that I love you and that

God will watch over you as He has done for me and for my father. You will be blessed. Carry on the family name after I am gone. Know that I have always been proud of you." Instead, the message was: "Go hunting, shoot some game, and make me a special dinner. Then, and only then, will I give you my blessing."

Faced with this condition, Esau left in search of game—and his father's blessing. At least hunting allowed Esau to use the skills that aided his self–esteem and confidence. But why did Esau even bother? Despite his resentment toward his parents, as evidenced in his choice of brides and in his cavalier attitude toward his birthright, Esau wanted the one thing he was never able to obtain—his father's unconditional love. So if it meant running all over the open country looking for game and going through the hassle of making a special dinner, it was worth it.

But while Isaac was instructing Esau, Rebekah was eavesdropping at the back of the tent. As soon as Esau went out to hunt, Rebekah ran to Jacob, her personal favorite, with a plot that would allow Jacob to receive Isaac's blessing. She told Jacob to bring her two young goats so she could fix the meat the way Isaac liked it. When Jacob brought in the food, Isaac would give Jacob the blessing first (see 27:5–10).

Jacob replied, "But my brother Esau is a hairy man, and I'm a man with smooth skin. What if my father touches me? I would appear to be tricking him and would bring down a curse on myself rather than a blessing" (27:11–12). Jacob's only concern was that he might not be able to pull off the deception. And if Isaac caught on, Jacob would be written out of the will, inheriting nothing—prophecy or no prophesy.

Corrupted by greed and ambition that benefitted her favorite son, Rebekah stood firm. "Let me worry about Isaac. You just do what I say." So sneaky Jake ran off to kill two goats, and Mama prepared the food. Gambling on Isaac's failing eyesight, Rebekah then swiped a set of Esau's best clothes for Jacob to wear and used the goatskin to cover the exposed skin on Jacob's hands and the back of his neck to complete the disguise. Both mother and son were ready to play out the lie.

Entering his father's tent with the platter of food, Jacob did his best impression of Esau's voice, "I am Esau your firstborn. I have done as you told me. Please sit up and eat some of my game so that you may give me your blessing" (27:19).

"Wow, that was fast. That deer must have been right outside the camp. Well done," Isaac may have said, obviously impressed by the delicious aroma filling the tent.

"The Lord your God gave me success," said Jacob (27:20). Not only was he lying, but he used God to give credibility to the fraud.

Blind but not senile, Isaac knew the deceitful natures of Jacob and Rebekah. He asked the boy to come closer to make sure it was Esau:

> "Come near so I can touch you, my son, to know whether you really are my son Esau or not." Jacob went close to his father Isaac, who touched him and said, "The voice is the voice of Jacob, but the hands are the hands of Esau" (27:21–22).

Isaac questioned the identity of his son once more, and again, Jacob insisted that he was Esau. Then Isaac's interest must have returned to his meal as he reiterated his *quid pro quo:* "My son, bring me some of your game to eat, so that I may give you my blessing" (27:25).

Things were going well. The old man ate and was happy, well fed, content, and eager to give his blessing. "Come here, my son, and kiss me" (27:26). Jacob came close and kissed his father. When Isaac caught the outdoorsy smell of Esau's clothes, he finally was convinced. "Ah, the smell of my son is like the smell of a field that the Lord has blessed" (27:27). A betrayal sealed with a kiss would happen again many years later in a garden, where one as close as a brother would "sell out" the Savior for thirty pieces of silver. Isaac proceeded to offer his blessing:

> May God give you of heaven's dew and of earth's richness—an abundance of grain and new wine. May nations serve you and peoples bow down to you. Be lord over your brothers, and may the sons of your mother bow down to you. May those who curse you be cursed and those who bless you be blessed (27:28–29).

Isaac made the mistake of trusting his son and his wife, and gave the blessing to Jacob. And once the blessing had been given, it could not be revoked. But how could it have happened? Did Isaac have such little dealings with his own sons that he lacked the instinctive ability to correctly identify them? Parents know their kids. We can distinguish their cries even as babies. The voices of our children are distinct to our ears—even in a crowd. Isaac, on the other hand, questioned his son's voice but allowed himself to be reassured by trickery.

In typical dysfunctional–parenting style, Isaac had chosen to avoid an active role in his sons' lives. He had not wanted to get involved in the squabbles between feuding siblings. Jacob and Esau had needed an interested participant for a dad; instead, they got Isaac. Human skin, goatskin—it's all the same. Obviously, Isaac had been more concerned about barbecue than about brothers.

And did Jacob have the slightest pang of remorse for the foul deed he had done to his father and brother? Did he ever consider what Esau's reaction might be? Maybe Jacob didn't care because he was blessed and there was nothing anyone could do about it.

As soon as Jacob had rushed out of Isaac's tent after scamming his way into the blessing, Esau returned from the hunt and prepared some "Cajun–style, extra spicy" venison barbecue. Eager for his parental approval, Esau said, "Father, sit up and eat some of my game, so that you may give me your blessing" (27:31). Maybe Isaac was lying down and sleepy after consuming the first massive helping.

Roused from his lethargy, Isaac asked, "What? Who are you?"

You can almost hear the impatience in Esau's voice as he replied, "I am your son, your firstborn, Esau."

Only then did Isaac realize what he had done. In a panic he trembled violently and said, "Who was it, then, that hunted game and brought it to me? I ate it just before you came and I blessed him—and indeed he will be blessed!" (27:33).

"When Esau heard his father's words, he burst out with a loud and bitter cry" (27:34). I imagine you could have heard his wailing all over the camp. Mothers brought their small children inside; grown men looked at each other in wonderment at such a mournful sound.

Isaac tried to explain, "Your brother came deceitfully and took your blessing" (27:35).

With rising fury Esau exclaimed, "Isn't he rightly named Jacob? [the supplanter] He has deceived me these two times: He took my birthright, and now he's taken my blessing!" In desperation Esau asked,

"Haven't you reserved any blessing for me?" (27:36).

Isaac replied, "I have made him lord over you and have made all his relatives his servants, and I have sustained him with grain and new wine. So what can I possibly do for you, my son?" (27:37).

Esau pleaded, "Do you have only one blessing, my father? Bless me too!" (27:38). Reeling from these great injustices from both brother and father, Esau wept uncontrollably. There was no blessing that Isaac would give. In fact, Isaac responded with a promise of violence, restlessness, poverty, and hardship:

> Your dwelling will be away from the earth's richness, away from the dew of heaven above. You will live by the sword and you will serve your brother. But when you grow restless, you will throw his yoke from off your neck (27:39–40).

Scripture then says, "Esau held a grudge against Jacob because of the blessing his father had given him" (27:41). This comment appears to be a bit understated. Esau's plan, in fact, was that once his father had died and the prescribed days of mourning were completed, he would get even—by killing Jacob and taking back his blessing one way or another. Jacob must have kept his face hidden around the camp, since Esau the hunter would have loved to have dropped his little brother with one well–placed arrow.

Rebekah, hearing of Esau's rage, warned Jacob to be on the alert: "Your brother Esau is consoling himself with the thought of killing you" (27:42). Even though there had been family precedents, fratricide was never looked upon as a favored method of settling sibling disputes. Rebekah quickly conceived yet another plan: "My son, do what I say: Flee at once to my brother Laban in Haran. Stay with him for a while until your brother's fury subsides. When your brother is no longer angry with you and forgets what you did to him, I'll send word for you to come back from there" (27:43–45). Did she actually think Esau would forget? But Rebekah's last comment is quite telling: "Why should I lose both of you in one day?" She knew she had already lost Esau because she had, in effect, chosen to abandon him.

Rebekah needed to protect her favored son. What she feared was that Esau would kill Jacob, and then Jacob's friends would kill Esau, and then a civil war would break out. In a culture familiar with blood feuds, killing members of rival factions occurred over much less than this. Wanting Jacob to hide out until the heat was off, she had to make it look like it was Isaac's idea so as not to further incriminate herself.

Rebekah said to Isaac, "I'm disgusted with living because of these Hittite women. If Jacob takes a wife from among the women of this land, from Hittite women like these, my life will not be worth living" (27:46)—another ruse, and a rather melodramatic one at that. She could not be less concerned about Jacob's ability to choose a wife because she trusted him. She was concerned, however, that Esau would find him and blow him away. If Jacob was an accomplished liar and a cheat, it was because he had a good coach—his mother.

She convinced her gullible husband that it was crucial to find a nice Hebrew girl for Jacob immediately, and the best place to do that was in the land where her father's house stood and where her brother Laban lived. After all, that is where Isaac's servant had found her. I imagine that Isaac wondered if he was being deceived. Did he, at this point, feel some degree of disgust at his own son and wife? Maybe he just felt used or stupid. Or did he worry that they might be willing to commit murder next to get what they wanted?

Isaac commanded Jacob not to even *think* about marrying a Canaanite woman. Then, almost parroting Rebekah's "suggestion," he told Jacob to "go at once to . . . the house of your mother's father Bethuel. Take a wife for yourself there, from among the daughters of Laban" (28:2). Isaac asked God to bless his son so that Jacob would fulfill the covenant the Lord had made with his family (see 28:3–4).

Hearing that Isaac had sent Jacob away to find a wife, Esau soon learned "how displeasing the Canaanite women were to his father" (28:8). So he decided to get even. Knowing that his Hittite wives were already a major source of familial conflict, Esau deliberately paid a visit to Ishmael in Canaan and married Mahalath, his daughter (see 28:9). Allied now with Ishmael against Isaac, the families were nearly guaranteed a long history of animosity. And through all of this turmoil, Isaac remained emotionally distant—and alone. But at least he had enjoyed his special meal. I hope it was worth it.

Chapter 12

Jacob

The Con Artist Gets Conned

As "Jacob left Beersheba and set out for Haran" (28:10), he knew that Esau was looking for him. It is likely that he loaded his camel in the dark, hoping the animal would not raise a ruckus as he made his escape. How ironic that the now–favored son and heir should have to steal away in the night like a common thief. But, a thief is what he was.

At the end of a long day's travel, Jacob made camp for the night. Since he had traded in his soft, warm bed for a life on the run, he used a rock for a pillow, and as he slept he had an incredible dream—a revelation from the Lord concerning the future. In the dream Jacob saw a stairway that went from earth all the way up to heaven with angels ascending and descending on it. At the top of the stairway he saw the Lord, who spoke and renewed the covenant with Abraham through Jacob just as He had with Isaac before him (see 28:12–15).

Jacob awoke terrified that he had unknowingly camped on holy ground (see 28:16–17). Knowing that mortal man cannot survive in God's presence and live, Jacob must have felt doubly afraid as he remembered that he had obtained Isaac's blessing by fraudulent means. Feeling a need to make amends, he took the stone he used for a pillow and set it up as a pillar, a stone of remembrance. He poured an offering of oil on it and changed the name of that place from Luz to Bethel, meaning "house of God." Grateful not to be reduced to ashes, he made a vow to the Lord.

> If God will be with me and will watch over me on this
> journey I am taking and will give me food to eat and
> clothes to wear so that I return safely to my father's house,
> then the Lord will be my God and this stone that I have
> set up as a pillar will be God's house, and of all that You
> give me I will give You a tenth (28:20–22).

In keeping with his upbringing of conditional love, it does seem in character for Jacob to set certain terms: *If God feeds, clothes, protects and blesses me, then I will allow God to be God and will tithe one tenth of all my goods.* Abraham had made the same offer without guarantees and gladly tithed without feeling obligated in any way. It was also easy for him to make that kind of promise when he was on the run and had nothing. But knowing Jacob's nature, to part with his tenth would undoubtedly be more difficult when he had wealth. We should not berate Jacob too much, however, for we all have done the same thing. We make lavish promises to repay God's kindness if He would only get us out of the fix we are in. But once the crisis passes, the promise is quickly forgotten.

Jacob went on his way, looking over his shoulder for any sign of Esau, until he arrived at a well in a field with three flocks of sheep nearby. "My brothers, where are you from?" he asked the shepherds.

"We're from Haran," they replied.

Hey, this is great, Jacob thought. *I have almost reached my destination.* He asked if they knew Laban, Nahor's grandson, and if he was well. They replied that indeed he was, and added that his daughter Rachel was approaching with her father's sheep just then. Jacob, taken with Rachel's beauty, rolled away the stone from the well and offered to water all her sheep. Again, Jacob would not have gone out of his way unless he saw profit of some kind to be gained—in this case, it was the heart of such an attractive woman (see 29:1–10). Wells seem to have been great places to meet girls. Just as Abraham's servant had found Rebekah, Jacob had also found a potential wife.

Scripture says that Jacob kissed Rachel and began to weep—with joy? with relief?—telling her that he was Rebekah's son and a relative of her father's. Rachel ran home to tell Laban the news. As soon as Laban heard that his nephew was at the well, he went to meet Jacob.

After they hugged and kissed and exchanged polite pleasantries about who was well, who was sick, and who was dead, Uncle Laban brought Jacob to his home and welcomed him with an apparently sincere "You are my own flesh and blood" (29:14).

When Jacob had been working for Laban and living with his family for a month, Laban took Jacob aside and said, "Just because you are a relative of mine, should you work for me for nothing? Tell me what your wages should be" (29:15). It first appears that Laban knew Jacob needed money to afford a wife, especially if that wife happened to be his daughter Rachel. Upon closer examination, however, Laban did not want to owe Jacob anything. If there was any owing to be done, it would be to Laban, for he was as cheap and sneaky as his nephew.

With little deliberation, Jacob specified the terms of his employment contract with Uncle Laban. Since he was deeply in love, he said, "I'll work for you seven years in return for your younger daughter Rachel" (29:18). In Jacob's mind, this seemed reasonable. He would earn the respect of the father of his bride–to–be, get the girl of his dreams, be allowed to see her every day, and have a safe place to live without having to watch his back. For Laban, the arrangement was as much a matter of control as it was one of finance. He got seven years of free labor, a dowry, and control over his employee. Since Jacob was a relative, all financial transactions would stay within the family; and as the prospective father of the bride, Laban figured that he might be in for another big payday from Isaac's heir. All in all, a great deal for both men—a win–win proposition.

Rachel was the first girl Jacob had met in Haran, and it was truly love at first sight—for Jacob, anyway. But Rachel had an older sister, Leah, who is described in the Bible as having "weak eyes" (29:17). We are not sure what the term "weak eyes" meant—myopic? droopy?—but the trait must have been noticeable enough to mention. I doubt, though, that Leah was unattractive except by comparison to Rachel.

"Jacob served seven years to get Rachel, but they seemed like only a few days to him because of his love for her" (29:20). When seven years had ended and Jacob was tired of cold showers, he told Laban, "Give me my wife. My time is completed" (29:21). A deal is a deal, and it was time for Jacob and Rachel to begin their lives as a married couple. So,

Laban threw a big party, inviting everyone to the wedding festivities.

Finally! After seven long years, Jacob had the chance to spend an intimate night with his new bride. (It was a good thing they waited, since in those days pre–marital fooling around was punishable with death by stoning.) Jacob must have had plenty to eat and drink at the celebration because the next morning when Jacob awoke with his bride in bed—surprise! It was Leah, not Rachel. Sometime during the feast, Laban had substituted sisters. To minimize the risk of having an unmarried daughter, it was the custom that younger sisters not marry before older ones. How ironic that Jacob, who disguised himself as his brother in order to swindle the blessing, was conned by Leah, who disguised herself as her sister. What goes around, comes around.

Furious doesn't begin to describe how Jacob must have felt at that moment. He screamed at Laban, "What is this you have done to me? I served you for Rachel, didn't I? Why have you deceived me?" (29:25). Isn't this always the way? People who make a history of dirty dealing are the first to cry "It's not fair!" when it happens to them. But Scripture is remarkably calm in its recording of Jacob's comments, for I imagine that his language may have been considerably more colorful. Frankly, I'm surprised he didn't have a stroke.

Laban explained that his actions were based on custom, and then he offered a counter–proposal. Urging Jacob not to humiliate Leah, who had probably been unfavorably compared to Rachel her entire life, he said, "Finish this daughter's bridal week; then we will give you the younger one also." In other words, just let Leah enjoy the week of bridal celebrations before she once again takes second place to Rachel—"in return for another seven years of work" (29:27). With this family, there was always a catch.

So Jacob did the right thing—at least once in his life—and made Leah feel honored and special. Laban also did the right thing in keeping his promise and giving Rachel to be Jacob's second wife. And after seven years, Jacob went from being single to having two wives within the span of less than two weeks. At least he would not have to spend the next seven years alone (29:28–29).

Jacob may have thought that his "family problems" were over—he had married the wife of his choice and he continued to work the full fourteen years of servitude to Laban in order to keep the peace. But peace was not in Jacob's future, for it was common knowledge that he loved Rachel more than he loved Leah, and playing favorites—as Jacob should have known—would cause great problems in the years to come.

The Race Is On

The Lord always has a way of leveling the playing field, for the Bible says, "When the Lord saw that Leah was not loved, He opened her womb, but Rachel was barren. Leah became pregnant and gave birth to a son. She named him Reuben, for she said, 'It is because the Lord has seen my misery. Surely my husband will love me now'" (29:31–32). Leah conceived again and gave birth to another son, Simeon, and said, "Because the Lord heard that I am not loved, He gave me this one too" (29:33). The Lord really must have loved Leah because she had a third son, Levi. She hoped, "Now at last my husband will become attached to me, because I have borne him three sons" (29:34). With the birth of her fourth son, Judah, she said, "This time I will praise the Lord" (29:35). But having children as a means of trying to win over a husband's love is just not a good idea.

Meanwhile, Jacob had no offspring by Rachel, the woman he did love—a family problem shared by Abraham and Sarah as well as Isaac and Rebekah. Unable to bear children, and not for lack of trying, Rachel became increasingly jealous of Leah. That must have been a first: Miss Perfect jealous of Miss Weak–Eyes! Rachel finally confronted Jacob in no uncertain terms: "Give me children, or I'll die!" (30:1).

Angrily Jacob responded, "Am I in the place of God, who has kept you from having children?" (30:2).

So Rachel resorted to a tactic used once before by Abraham and Sarah, repeating a pattern that had nearly resulted in tragedy. She turned to a surrogate to begin a family of her own. Rachel offered Jacob her maid–servant Bilhah to take as a wife: "Sleep with her so that she can bear children for me and that through her I too can build a family" (30:3). So he did, and she did, and they had a son. Rachel named the boy Dan, exclaiming, "God has vindicated me; He has listened to my plea and given me a son" (30:6).

Bilhah conceived again and had another son that Rachel named Naphtali, which means "my struggle." Rachel claimed, "I have had a great struggle with my sister, and I have won" (see 30:7–8).

So the competition was on, and Rachel—with the help of Bilhah—was catching up! This prolific bunch was, in fact, just getting warmed up, as they tried—all by themselves—to fulfill the prophecy that Abraham's descendants would be as numerous as the grains of sand on the seashore.

This rivalry between sisters soon reached crisis proportions as they jockeyed for Jacob's affection. Leah discovered that she was no longer able to bear children herself, so she gave her servant Zilpah to be Jacob's fourth wife. Zilpah promptly conceived and added yet another son to the family. "What good fortune!" Leah exclaimed, and named him Gad, which can mean either "good fortune" or "a troop" (30:9–11). In short order, Zilpah also had Asher, which means "happy."

"How happy I am! The women will call me happy," delighted Leah, who was way ahead in the son count (30:12–13). But she wasn't done yet—not by a long–shot.

At this point, Jacob was wondering what he had gotten himself into. At least the teams of competing wives were even!

During the wheat harvest, Jacob's firstborn, Reuben, came across some mandrake plants, a supposed Middle Eastern fertility enhancer. He brought them home to his mother Leah, but Aunt Rachel found out about the mandrakes and said to Leah, "Please give me some of your son's mandrakes" (30:14). The days of sisterly cooperation were over, however, and every comment or request was perceived as a threat to be rebuffed at all cost.

Leah replied, no doubt with an accusing and sarcastic edge to her voice, "Wasn't it enough that you took away my husband? Will you take my son's mandrakes too?" (30:15). In negotiating a bartered payment for the mandrakes, Rachel allowed Leah to have sex that night with Jacob, since apparently it was not yet her turn. So when Jacob returned from the fields, Leah told him of the arrangement, and she and Jacob made their marital rendezvous.

Sure enough, Leah was back in the baby business! She had a fifth son named Issachar (which sounds like "reward" in Hebrew) because

"God has rewarded me for giving my maidservant to my husband" (30:18). After that she had a sixth son, Zebulun, saying, "God has presented me with a precious gift. This time my husband will treat me with honor, because I have borne him six sons" (30:20). Just to break the pattern of boys in the family, Leah had a daughter next, Dinah. One day that little lady would have an interesting story of her own.

Just in case you have lost count, Leah had six boys and one girl; Zilpah and Bilhah had two sons apiece, giving Jacob a total of eleven children. Rachel still had none, but "then God remembered Rachel; He listened to her and opened her womb. She became pregnant and gave birth to a son and said, 'God has taken away my disgrace.' She named him Joseph" (30:22–24). And although the sons of Leah, Zilpah, and Bilhah were numerous, none were called by God for His service like Rachel's son, Joseph, would be one day.

A Lesson in Ancient Genetics

More than fourteen years had passed since Jacob had run away from Esau, and he might have thought that it was safe to return home with his abundant progeny. So after Joseph was born, Jacob felt the need to return to his homeland. He said to Laban, "Give me my wives and children, for whom I have served you, and I will be on my way. You know how much work I've done for you" (30:26).

Jacob had done well by Laban, building his herds of livestock so that Laban prospered in the sheep business. Knowing a good thing when he saw it, Laban was reluctant to let Jacob and his brood leave. He knew the Lord had brought prosperity to his business because of Jacob—not because of anything Laban had done. He never had an employee or relative who worked harder or smarter. Laban decided to bargain: "Name your wages, and I will pay them" (30:28).

The last time Laban had asked a question like that, Jacob had asked for Rachel in marriage. But instead, Jacob got Leah, and things were never calm again. Needless to say, Jacob was skeptical. But seeing an opportunity for his own financial gain, Jacob replied:

> If you will do this one thing for me, I will go on tending
> your flocks and watching over them: Let me go through

> all your flocks today and remove from them every speck-
> led or spotted sheep, every dark–colored lamb and every
> spotted or speckled goat. They will be my wages. And my
> honesty will testify for me in the future, whenever you
> check on the wages you have paid me. Any goat in my
> possession that is not speckled or spotted, or any lamb
> that is not dark–colored, will be considered stolen
> (30:31–33).

Jacob would tend the rest of Laban's flocks as before, except that all the speckled and dark–colored sheep and goats would be removed from the area and kept for himself.

At this point, most of the flocks must have been solid and light in color, so Laban figured that he would not have to part with too many. He agreed to the deal. But what gradually occurred is a strange lesson in pre–Gregor Mendel genetics: During the mating seasons, Jacob cut and peeled tree branches to look like stripes. He then placed them at the watering troughs at eye level to the animals so that they would mate directly in front of the striped branches—as if to plant in the animals' minds a pattern of stripes rather than solid colors! Whenever there was a young one born speckled, spotted, or dark, Jacob would stash that sheep or goat far away from Laban's flocks. Jacob also bred the strongest, most desirable animals with his own stock, while the weaker animals were mated with Laban's.

Jacob's idea was sound, even if his understanding of genetics was not. Keeping and breeding the strongest does make for a healthier, more prolific flock, and combining the genetic traits of the solid–color breeds also increases the probability of having speckled sheep and goats. As a result, Jacob became a prosperous man of prestige, as increasingly more livestock were born not of a solid color (see 30:37–43).

Once Jacob began amassing sheep and goats at a faster rate than anyone in the region, he could not help but notice how Laban's attitude was changing. Laban may have been cheap, but he certainly was not stupid—and neither were his own sons, in charge of the day–to–day operations in the sheep business. It did not take long for them to see Jacob's net worth increasing as theirs held steady or declined. What really bothered them was not that Jacob was doing well, but that his success came at their expense. His ovine assets represented their lost inheritance (see 31:1). This growing resentment over livestock would be the catalyst for the move back to Canaan.

The Final Showdown

God said to Jacob, "Go back to the land of your fathers and to your relatives, and I will be with you" (31:3). So Jacob sent for Rachel and Leah to meet him in the fields where his flocks were, away from Laban's informants. There, he shared his perspective on the whole situation with his wives, who had put aside their petty grievances of each other for the time being:

> I see that your father's attitude toward me is not what it was before, but the God of my father has been with me. You know that I've worked for your father with all my strength, yet your father has cheated me by changing my wages ten times. However, God has not allowed him to harm me. . . . So God has taken away your father's livestock and has given them to me (31:5–7,9).

Jacob then informed Rachel and Leah of God's command to leave. The wives listened and realized, "Hey, is Dad going to take everything you earned for him? By rights, all of this should belong to us and our kids. If God told you to go, Jacob, then we're outta here!" (see 31:14–16). For the first time, the feuding wives spoke in terms of "us" and "our" instead of "me" and "mine." Were they finally thinking and acting like a family—or were they just protecting their own investments? Either way, Laban would not be happy.

With as little commotion as possible, Jacob prepared to go back to Canaan. He knew that Laban would try to renegotiate, use a stalling tactic, or even lay a guilt trip on the family, so he planned to be long gone by the time Laban discovered they had left. When Laban had gone off for several days to shear his sheep, they made their getaway with all their livestock and belongings. But Rachel ran back to Laban's tent and stole his household idols, which he believed helped provide pasture, rain, and fertile breeding stock (see 31:17–19).

Laban had to be told that Jacob had fled with the family, and by that time, the runaways had a three–day head start (see 31:22). Laban took off—in pursuit of Jacob and daughters and grandkids. (Or was he really in pursuit of the herds and household idols?) It took seven days, but Laban finally caught up with them in the hill country of Gilead.

The night before Laban's planned confrontation, God came to him in a dream and said, "Be careful not to say anything to Jacob, either good or bad" (31:24). The Lord understood Laban's heart and knew that nothing good would come of his bluster or threats. But when they met, Laban couldn't help but fire the opening salvo:

> What have you done? You've deceived me, and you've car-
> ried off my daughters like captives in war. Why did you
> run off secretly and deceive me? Why didn't you tell me,
> so I could send you away with joy and singing to the
> music of tambourines and harps? You didn't even let me
> kiss my grandchildren and my daughters good–by. You
> have done a foolish thing (31:26–28).

That was what he said. It was the guilt–trip approach. But what he meant was: *Keep the brats. I never did like them anyway. And you can have my daughters with my compliments. But I want the sheep that are rightfully mine and anything else of value you swiped before you ran off like the stinking, low–life slug I always took you for.*

Sensing that Jacob was unruffled by the attempts at false affection and guilt, Laban threw out an idle threat ("I have the power to harm you") then played his final card: "Why did you steal my gods?" (31: 29–30). Jacob calmly told Laban the truth as to why he had left so secretly—it was because he was afraid Laban would take his family away from him by force.

As to the matter of the household gods, Jacob confidently stated, "If you find anyone who has your gods, he shall not live. In the pres-ence of our relatives, see for yourself whether there is anything of yours here with me; and if so, take it" (31:32). Jacob obviously was unaware that his favorite wife had "clipped" the idols. So Laban began a tent–by–tent search of Jacob's camp. He rummaged through every-thing but did not find the missing items. When he came to Rachel's tent, Laban tore up the place looking in every container. But she had hidden the idols in her camel's saddle and was sitting on them throughout the search. To avoid any suspicion, Rachel said quite demurely to her father, "Don't be angry, my lord, that I cannot stand up in your presence; I'm having my period" (31:35). Unable to find his lost property, Laban gave up the search.

By now Jacob had recovered his ire over this blatant intrusion into his personal affairs, and he fired back: "What is my crime? . . . What sin have I committed that you hunt me down? Now that you have searched through all my goods, what have you found that belongs to your household? Put it here in front of your relatives and mine, and let them judge between the two of us" (31:36–37). In other words, *show me the evidence or get out of my face!*

Jacob continued, venting years of repressed rage:

> I have been with you for twenty years now. Your sheep and goats have not miscarried, nor have I eaten rams from your flocks. I did not bring you animals torn by wild beasts; I bore the loss myself. And you demanded payment from me for whatever was stolen by day or night. This was my situation: The heat consumed me in the daytime and the cold at night, and sleep fled from my eyes. It was like this for the twenty years I was in your household. I worked for you fourteen years for your two daughters and six years for your flocks, and you changed my wages ten times. If the God of my father, the God of Abraham and the Fear of Isaac, had not been with me, you would surely have sent me away empty–handed. But God has seen my hardship and the toil of my hands, and last night He rebuked you (31:38–42).

Take that, you old cheapskate!

Not one to be bested in an argument, Laban tried a retort that claimed ownership to his daughters, his grandchildren, and to the flocks. This line of reasoning was shaky at best since he had made numerous agreements with Jacob in front of many witnesses. Had he tried to take back what he thought was his by force, Laban would have started a war. War with Jacob would have been difficult; war with his daughters, impossible. Realizing he had no other alternative but to cut his losses, Laban called for a truce. As was the practice of the time, Jacob and his relatives erected a pile of stones to serve as a permanent marker of their pact. Laban called the place Jegar Sahadutha, and Jacob called it Galeed. Both names, in Aramaic and Hebrew, mean, "witness heap" because Laban said, "This heap is a witness between you and me today" (see 31:43–48).

The pile of stones has also been called *Mizpah* (watchtower) through the ages since Laban also said to Jacob, "May the Lord keep watch between you and me when we are away from each other. If you mistreat my daughters or if you take any wives besides my daughters, even though no one is with us, remember that God is a witness between you and me" (31:49–50). More than a marker to honor a pact, the pile further denoted a line of demarcation, much like the 38th parallel that separates North and South Korea today. Upon what little was left of his honor, Laban declared, "This heap is a witness . . . that I will not go past this heap to your side to harm you and that you will not go past . . . to my side to harm me. May the God of Abraham and the God of Nahor, the God of their father, judge between us" (31:52–53).

The situation ended without violence, as sacrifices were offered to the Lord and to Laban's purloined household deities *in absentia*. After sharing a last big family meal and spending the night, Laban kissed his daughters and grandchildren, gave them his parting blessing, and left for home in the morning. Jacob also continued his journey with the family, satisfied with what had been a peaceful resolution. But as he got closer to Canaan and home, he knew he still had to face brother Esau.

Chapter 13

Jacob Confronts His Past

Return of the Cheat

Fans of "Star Trek" know the ancient Klingon proverb: "Revenge is a dish best served cold." In Esau's case, revenge was nothing if not blazing hot, for he had lost his birthright, his blessing, and his inheritance by conspiracy, deception, and fraud—all perpetrated by his own brother. One would hope, however, that animosity between brothers had abated after twenty years. But Esau had been resolute in his intent to find Jacob and kill him. The truth is that entire countries have been known to feud for centuries over issues such as those of Jacob and Esau—ancient disputes that few can remember in detail.

Jacob enjoyed his wealth, his large family, and a few other tangible benefits of Isaac's blessing. But he would not find lasting solace within himself until he confronted his past and made peace with Esau. Saying "I was ill–advised" would not work; neither would "I was mistaken." Only the words "I was wrong and am so sorry" and the willingness to make amends would do. In order to fully realize the blessing, Jacob knew he needed closure.

One of the things that marks our modern society is the desire for closure. We may experience pain and sorrow but want it concluded so we can "move on." Much of this comes from our instantaneous news media that desires to package information and life experience into neat thirty–second segments. We can grieve, laugh, or cry for a time, but then we want it concluded with no loose ends. It is not so much that the people who are experiencing grief want closure, but those who have to witness or report it, just want the whole thing to go away.

Closure can be part of a healing process if apologies are expressed and amends are made, but the first step in that process is to admit responsibility for what has happened. This was true for Jacob. The Lord had allowed him to prosper, but until he came before his brother in humility and repentance, he would not find lasting security.

After parting ways with Laban, Jacob sent messengers ahead to locate Esau in the land of Seir in Edom. He wanted to find Esau and beg his forgiveness before Esau caught sight of the massive caravan marching into Canaan. Once they found Esau, the messengers were to inform him that brother Jacob was coming—and bringing abundance to be shared as a gesture of goodwill. The message was celebratory yet humble:

> I have been staying with Laban and have remained there till now. I have cattle and donkeys, sheep and goats, menservants and maidservants. Now I am sending this message to my lord, that I may find favor in your eyes (32:4–5).

Was it really a gesture of goodwill or a bribe to keep Esau from carrying out his vendetta? Jacob would soon find out, for when the messengers returned from their errand, they said, "We went to your brother Esau, and now he is coming to meet you, *and four hundred men are with him*" (32:6). That must have sounded rather ominous to Jacob. Not only was Esau coming to him, but he was leading a huge posse! What was intended to be a message of reconciliation was beginning to feel like an invitation to a massacre.

Responding to this possible threat, "in great fear and distress Jacob divided the people who were with him into two groups, and the flocks and herds and camels as well" (32:7). His rational thinking was that if one group was attacked, the other might escape safely, and some sons might survive to carry on the family line and complete the prophecy of a perpetual inheritance. But Jacob also may have finally understood his responsibilities as the carrier of the covenant when he prayed.

O Lord . . . I am unworthy of all the kindness and faithfulness You have shown Your servant. I had only my staff
when I crossed this Jordan, but now I have become two
groups. Save me, I pray, from the hand of my brother
Esau, for I am afraid he will come and attack me, and also
the mothers with their children. But You have said, "I will
surely make you prosper and will make your descendants
like the sand of the sea, which cannot be counted"
(32:9–12).

With a sense of inner calm that could only have been described as
a gift from God, Jacob retired for the night and prepared suitable gifts
for Esau—hundreds of head of a variety of prime livestock—a very
substantial gift from a man used to getting rather than giving. But I
imagine Jacob thought survival was well worth the expense. Jacob sent
each herd ahead, in the care of a trusted servant who was instructed to
say to Esau when they met, "[These animals] belong to your servant
Jacob. They are a gift sent to my lord Esau" (32:18). It was also crucial
for each servant to add, "Your servant Jacob is coming behind us"
(32:20). Jacob was hoping that all these herds would pacify Esau by the
time the brothers reached each other.

Under cover of darkness Jacob's family crossed along a ford in the
Jabbok River so they would not be harmed if things got dangerous.
After they crossed safely, Jacob sent over all his possessions. Before he
could leave and join the rest, Scripture says he wrestled with a man all
night until daybreak. We can only speculate that "the man" Jacob
wrestled with was an angel of God or perhaps the pre–incarnate Christ.
What were they fighting about? Was Jacob trying to leave, and the man
would not let him cross the river to rejoin the rest, or was Jacob trying
to keep the man from leaving? Did Jacob think he was one of Esau's hit
men who had arrived to "make him an offer he couldn't refuse?" The
Bible seems deliberately unspecific, but it does say that "Jacob was left
alone," implying that he was undistracted by any earthly disturbance
and may have been finally forced to come to terms with himself.

When it became clear that neither combatant could overpower the
other, the mysterious man "touched the socket of Jacob's hip so that his

hip was wrenched as he wrestled with the man" (32:25). That little wrestling move dropped Jacob to his knees, so that all he could do was hang on to the stranger and not let go. Jacob demanded, "I will not let you go unless you bless me" (32:26).

The stranger replied with neither blessing nor curse, but asked Jacob his name. When Jacob answered, the man said, "Your name will no longer be Jacob, but Israel, because you have struggled with God and with men and have overcome" (32:28).

What did Jacob think at this point: *I have just wrestled with God and am not dead? No, really. Who IS this man?* Jacob asked for his name again but the stranger questioned Jacob, "Why do you ask my name?" In other words, *Don't you already know, Silly?* Then he blessed Jacob, now named Israel, and left as mysteriously as he had come (see 32:29).

The visitor had wrestled with Jacob to demonstrate how Jacob had manipulated people and situations for his own benefit. But it was time for Jacob to learn that God was in charge. The Lord could either disable him with a simple touch or shower him with gracious abundance, and Jacob had to succumb to that knowledge. Jacob must have felt content, however, in knowing that he put up a good fight and that the Lord was pleased with his personal growth. (God would not reveal His name to mankind until Moses asked the same question and received the answer "I AM"—not "I was" or "I will be," but have always been and always will be—all-powerful, self-sustaining, and perfect.)

Weary, sweaty, and sore, Jacob knew he had been in the presence of God—twice—and lived to tell the tale. He called the place of his struggle Peniel, meaning "face of God." But Jacob did not have much time to revel in his encounter or tell his family of the adventure. No sooner had he limped past Peniel and crossed the ford than he saw brother Esau coming with his 400 men—and he could not tell if Esau wanted to settle the score or not. He reacted by putting the kids in order—Zilpah and Bilhah's children in front, then Leah and her brood, and behind them Rachel and Joseph. That certainly would have been a sign to the wives and children as to Dad's loyalties. He protected Rachel and Joseph while exposing the others to face the brunt of the fight if it came to that. Then Jacob went out ahead of the rest to face Esau.

In a gesture of deference and respect, Jacob bowed seven times as he approached his brother. As he looked up, Jacob saw Esau running toward him. Perhaps he braced for the thrust of the blade that might be coming, or looked to see if his children were safe or if there was a way of escape. He might have thought, *This is it. He's coming and there is nowhere to run!* Might the hip injury have been the Lord's way of anchoring Jacob to the spot to make sure he did not revert to his usual pattern of running away from a crisis?

But Jacob did not have to run, for rather than pulling a knife, Esau embraced his brother, kissed him, and they both wept openly at the long–anticipated reunion. After the hugging had subsided, Esau looked Jacob over once or twice and then noticed all the women and children who had gathered.

"Who are these with you?" Esau asked.

Quite formally, keeping a suitable tone of submission, as he did not yet fully know Esau's intentions, Jacob responded, "They are the [wives and] children God has graciously given your servant" (33:5).

One by one, the entire family filed in to be introduced, each one bowing to Uncle Esau starting with Bilhah's and Zilpah's children and continuing all the way to Rachel and Joseph. The mothers must have coached the kids to mind their manners and not to say anything rude or stupid, for Esau was like a lion on a leash—restrained and friendly— but a lion nonetheless, capable of making life extremely uncomfortable should he have chosen to do so.

"Reuben, Simeon, Judah, Gad, Asher, Issachar, Naphtali, Levi, Dan, Zebulon, Dinah, Joseph, . . . Dopey, Sleepy, Sneezy, Bashful, . . . Comet, Cupid, Donner, Blitzen, . . . say hello to your Uncle Esau."

"Hello, Uncle Esau," came the reply in unison from the chorus of Jacobic progeny.

Esau abruptly changed the subject: "What's the deal with all the livestock and your men saying that they all belong to you?" inquiring about the herds moving across the countryside like a western cattle drive headed for Dodge City.

"Those are gifts for you, to find favor in your eyes, my lord," Jacob replied (see 33:8).

"But Esau said, 'I already have plenty, my brother. Keep what you have for yourself.'"

"'No, please!' said Jacob. 'If I have found favor in your eyes, accept this gift from me. For to see your face is like seeing the face of God, now that you have received me favorably'" (33:9–10). How true that the look of affection and acceptance from Esau reminded Jacob of seeing the face of God, accepting and affectionate in His blessing at daybreak.

After a few go–rounds like two men insisting on who picks up the check for dinner, Esau finally relented and accepted the gifts. I guess he decided it was best not to look a gift camel in the mouth. And Jacob was, at last, showing signs of the Lord at work in his life. In the old days, Jacob would have given Esau the gifts and then devised a plan to steal them back, while justifying the theft and making it look like Esau's fault.

Esau offered to accompany his brother back to Seir, but Jacob was unable to travel as fast as Esau might have liked because of the children and the young livestock. "Let my lord go on ahead of his servant, while I move along slowly at the pace of the droves before me and that of the children" (33:14). So Esau then recommended that he leave some of his men to help with the caravan, but Jacob demurred, saying, "But why do that? . . . Just let me find favor in the eyes of my lord" (33:15). Having made amends with his brother, Jacob needed nothing more. Parting company, Esau returned to Seir and Jacob went on to Succoth, where he built temporary housing for his people and corrals for all his animals to rest from the rigors of cross–country travel.

Jacob's journey was almost at an end when the troops camped in Canaan within sight of the city of Shechem. Needing to establish a sense of permanence, he bought a parcel of land and immediately erected an altar to the Lord, calling it *El Elohe Israel* (see 33:18–20). He would need that place to pray, for things were going to get complicated again because of his one daughter, Dinah.

Dinah and the Shechemites

Being the only sister with eleven brothers, Dinah was one of the most protected young ladies who ever lived. A young suitor would have to be an exceptional specimen of manhood, indeed, to survive the weeding–out process—not only by the brothers but especially by the dad. When it comes to dating, dads have a special interest in keeping their darling daughters away from any sex–crazed, testosterone–driven boys, remembering that they were once exactly the same. Being the father of a daughter brings all kinds of interesting challenges, since it has been demonstrated time after time that girls often marry a man like their father. If Dad is loving, attentive, kind, and strong, they will have a better chance of gravitating to someone with the same qualities, just as surely as they will be drawn to the opposite.

Scripture says that Dinah, the daughter of Jacob and Leah, took a stroll one day to visit the women of the land. She probably needed some female companionship to give balance to her life. While out with the girls, she was sexually assaulted by Shechem, son of Hamor the Hivite, ruler of that part of Canaan. According to Scripture, Shechem had seen Dinah and immediately "his heart was drawn to [her]." Apparently, he had fallen in love but had a brutal way of showing it. We do not know if the feeling was mutual or if the encounter was consensual, but when the narration uses the words "violated" and "defiled," logic tells us that the use of force, or at least coercion, occurred. And in any culture, under any circumstance, unwanted sexual advances are always wrong. Romance and love never mix with the act of rape, for rape is an act of aggression, not affection. Shechem then went to his father and said, "Get me this girl as my wife" (34:4). Was Dinah to become one of several wives, or was she to be the first?

When Jacob heard about the assault, his sons were in the fields. So Dad kept the matter quiet until they got home, perhaps so that he could hold a family meeting to decide what to do about this insult to the honor of his daughter—and to the family of Israel. Sending for the lads might have provoked a bloodbath. As soon as Jacob's sons heard what had happened, they were ripping mad and ready to get even (see 34:7). Were they actually more upset by what had happened to their sister— or at the insult that the Canaanites had inflicted on them? Were they defending their sister's honor or their own?

Shechem's father Hamor came to Jacob to see if some arrangement could be made for his son to marry Dinah. Never in the negotiations was an apology given for the violation. In Hamor's eyes, there was no problem. His son liked the girl, wanted to marry her, and was willing to pay Jacob and the boys a fair price to arrange the marriage:

> My son Shechem has his heart set on your daughter. Please give her to him as his wife. Intermarry with us; give us your daughters and take our daughters for yourselves. You can settle among us; the land is open to you. Live in it, trade in it, and acquire property in it (34:8–10).

But the phrase "intermarry with us," buried in the middle of Hamor's innocent–sounding plea in defense of young love, betrayed his true intent. If they intermarried, then future generations would blur the distinctions that separated them. Eventually Hebrews would worship the pantheon of Canaanite deities and develop new families who would take spiritual and emotional priority over the covenant with God that dated back to Abraham.

Then Shechem made his own plea, trying to bring the focus back to issues of power and money. He allowed Dinah's father and brothers to "make the price for the bride and the gift I am to bring as great as you like, and I'll pay whatever you ask me" (see 34:11–12).

Still smarting from the collective insult to the family honor, Dinah's brothers would not be so easily swayed. Their interest was not to gain more wealth but to get even. The boys conspired among themselves to take revenge. When asked if Shechem could marry Dinah, the older lads replied:

> We can't do such a thing; we can't give our sister to a man who is not circumcised. That would be a disgrace to us. We will give our consent to you on one condition only: that you become like us by circumcising all your males. Then we will give you our daughters and take your daughters for ourselves. We'll settle among you and become one people with you. But if you will not agree to be circumcised, we'll take our sister and go (34:14–17).

The proposal seemed reasonable. The Hivites considered the rite of circumcision to be merely a Hebrew thing done to please God. But since they did not believe in Him anyway, what was the harm? It might be somewhat painful and inconvenient, but it was worth it to Shechem to marry Dinah, and worth it to Hamor to absorb the Hebrews into Canaanite society. And if all males were circumcised, there would be no visible difference between Hebrew or pagan. At this point, love–struck Shechem would have agreed to anything short of death to keep Dinah in his house.

Hamor and Shechem wasted no time in presenting the proposal to their fellow townsmen: "Let them live in our land and trade in it; the land has plenty of room for them. We can marry their daughters and they can marry ours. . . . Won't their livestock, their property and all their other animals become ours? So let us give our consent to them [to be circumcised], and they will settle among us" (34:21–23). So the males all agreed to be circumcised like their Hebrew neighbors. But they discovered the procedure was far more painful than they had estimated. Afterwards, they were all home mending, doing nothing more strenuous than reading or sleeping. No one was in any mood to go to work—and certainly not in any condition to go to war.

Simeon and Levi, two of Dinah's brothers, waited three days after the mass operations and then attacked the city, killing every defenseless male and specifically targeting Hamor and Shechem. (I doubt that this plan of revenge was accomplished by only two men, regardless of how incapacitated their opponents were. But Joseph was probably too young to be involved in the fighting.) As Simeon and Levi took Dinah home, the rest of the brothers came and looted the city, seizing all the livestock, and carrying off the women and children along with their belongings (see 34:25–29).

When Jacob got the news of the massacre, he was livid. But his reaction was not to the fact that his boys had killed defenseless people, stolen property, and made women widows and children orphans. Jacob was angry because they had made him look bad. He said to Simeon and Levi, "You have brought trouble on me by making me a stench to the Canaanites and Perizzites, the people living in this land. We are few in number, and if they join forces against me and attack me, I and my household will be destroyed" (34:30). To paraphrase, "You have brought trouble on *me*, making *me* a stench. If they join forces against *me*, then *my* household will be destroyed." Me, me, me. And we thought Jacob had allowed the Lord to change his nature into someone generous and thoughtful, but he was still as egocentric as always. Feeling doubly betrayed, Jacob's sons responded defensively, "Should he [Shechem] have treated our sister like a prostitute?" (34:31). They were outraged by Shechem's assault on their sister, but they were more furious that Jacob had done nothing to remedy the situation other than try to turn a profit on an arranged marriage. Accusations must have flown back and forth until the Lord finally intervened and told Jacob and his family to leave the land of Canaan and return to Bethel, where He had first appeared to Jacob.

When we strike off in a direction away from God and eventually get lost in the process, going back to where we first experienced God's presence is good advice. When we return to the place where we once lived close to the Lord's guidance, we find ourselves again on solid footing. God wanted Jacob where he had been truly dependent on God, not on his own creativity or cunning. When Jacob had been scared and on the run, at Bethel his heart was tender. At Bethel, Jacob had needed God, and there he would need Him again.

In the Spirit of Inner Cleansing

Jacob understood that the Lord did not want his extended family getting attached to pagan ways through their associations with the Shechemites and other Canaan tribes. Before the entire tribe hit the road, Jacob told them they needed to do some spiritual housekeeping and remove all sources of temptation. He said, "Get rid of the foreign gods you have with you, and purify yourselves and change your clothes. Then come, let us go up to Bethel, where I will build an altar to God, who answered me in the day of my distress and who has been with me wherever I have gone" (35:2–3). They were to dispose of any idols they had made or accumulated—even the ones Rachel had swiped from her father. And in purifying themselves, they needed to get rid of their earrings, for it was the custom of both males and females in the Canaanite tribes to wear earrings. They were items of great personal pride, and the relative value of their jewelry was a reflection of their social status and wealth.

By the way, it was the Hebrew wives, sons, and daughters who gave Aaron their earrings to make the Golden Calf, while Moses was on Mount Sinai receiving the law from God (see Exodus 31:18–32:7). And later in history, when Gideon wanted to celebrate his triumph over the Midianites, he asked each of his men to contribute an earring from their share of the plunder to make an ephod (see Judges 8:22–27). It seems that Jacob's descendants have created several problems for themselves with idols and earrings. But the issue has never been with the earring itself but with the false gods.

The Lord wanted Jacob's family to distinguish themselves from the tribes of Canaan—in appearance and in action. By keeping the idols and trinkets of a prior lifestyle, they would risk a regression in their spiritual development. So Jacob buried all of the castoff objects under a big oak tree in Shechem.

In J. R. R. Tolkien's *The Lord of the Rings,* Frodo must take the one ring of evil power to the volcano, where it was forged, to destroy it. In much the same way, Jacob and his family had to bury their idols, take off their earrings, and change their clothes. They were making a new start, and they could not survive and grow to be God's people if they continued to play with forbidden things.

When the surrounding tribes learned what had happened to the Shechemites following Dinah's assault and heard that Jacob's family was leaving, "the terror of God fell upon the towns all around them so that no one pursued them" (35:5). So the group made it to Bethel, and Jacob built an altar called El Bethel "because it was there that God revealed Himself to him [Jacob] when he was fleeing from his brother" (35:7). In Bethel, Jacob could offer sacrifice and worship God with a clear conscience—perhaps for the first time in years. But while there, Rebekah's nurse, Deborah, died (35:8). The Bible then repeats what had occurred to Jacob—how God had appeared to him, reminding him of the promises of God's covenant (see 35:9–15).

Rachel's Death and Reuben's Indiscretion

As was the practice with nomadic shepherds, Jacob's family never stayed in one place for too long, always in need of fresh pasture and water. During a move from Bethel to Ephrath, Rachel was expecting her second child, but while still some distance from the town of Ephrath, Rachel went into labor—and things did not go well. Rachel died of undisclosed complications, yet she lived long enough to name her son Ben–Oni (son of my trouble). Jacob called him Benjamin (see 35:16–18). How did Rachel's death affect Jacob? Had he pleaded with God to spare her life? Did he harbor resentment or blame the Lord? Jacob buried Rachel along the trail and erected a pillar to hallow the spot. She had been the mother of Joseph and Benjamin—two lads who would find a special place of honor with their father. Jacob's ten other sons, however, soon felt like second–class citizens. Just as Isaac and Rebekah had played the favorite–child game, Jacob began to repeat the same pattern, giving preferential treatment to Joseph and Benjamin at the expense of the others. Being the youngest, Benjamin probably became an over–protected child like his grandfather Isaac.

The family was growing up, and a whole new generation of dysfunctional behavior was developing. Reuben, Jacob's eldest, acquired a sense of power and virility as his father aged. As the firstborn, he would receive the family blessing for himself. Wanting to make this point clear, perhaps, Reuben decided to have sex with Bilhah, Jacob's third wife. Since he would one day own everything of his father's anyway, he thought he might just get a head start (see 35:22). Was Reuben demonstrating an act of defiance, or was this his odd way of getting his father's attention since Jacob was so absorbed with grief for Rachel? (I wonder how Reuben broke the news to Dan and Naphtali—"Guess what, guys? I had sex with your mom!" In my neighborhood any comment about somebody's mother was a sure way to start a riot.)

Did Reuben openly flaunt the affair, daring his father to try and stop him? Was the old man disappointed? Outraged? Scripture does not state any reaction on Jacob's part. And unlike the description of Dinah's sexual encounter, nothing indicates that Bilhah was anything other than a willing participant. How did this influence her relationship with Jacob and the other wives? Would she have appeared somehow more favorable? I doubt that her behavior endeared her to Leah, Zilpah, or the other children. There is a lot we will never know, but one thing we do know is that Reuben would never be the primary son despite his assumptions to the contrary.

Lost Opportunities

After years of travel, adventures, multiple wives, children, and a life filled with spiritual highs and lows, Jacob and his brood came home to his father Isaac in Mamre, where the family burial plot was located. How wonderful for Isaac to have witnessed the scheming son return with so much to show for his life, especially since Isaac had so little to show for his own. According to the Bible, Isaac lived to be 180, and then he "was gathered to his people" as brothers Jacob and Esau buried him (see 35:27–29).

Although one of the "big three" listed in Scripture—Abraham, Isaac, and Jacob—Isaac is dropped from the biblical narrative when Jacob runs away to Uncle Laban until the point of his death. Once Isaac was duped by the whole brother/blessing switcheroo, he and Rebekah are essentially written out of the story. Rebekah is not mentioned again until Genesis chapter 49, where she is listed as one of those interred in the family cemetery. There is no mention of her death or any other information about her, but it is likely that Rebekah died before Isaac.

Remember the reference to the death of Deborah, Rebekah's nurse? If Rebekah was dead and no longer in need of personal care, Deborah, lacking family of her own after giving years of devoted service to Rebekah's family, may well have left Isaac's employ to serve Jacob and family. (From what I have studied of Jacob, he was a continual work in progress, who might have benefitted from full–time supervision.)

Once old Isaac had figured out Esau and Rebekah's entire plot, I cannot help but think that Rebekah was *persona non grata* in her own household, as the two simply drifted farther and farther apart. Would the years have softened the memories of opportunities lost, or would Isaac and Rebekah have just gotten old, lonely, and bitter until they ran out of days to make things right? For two young people with such great potential—Isaac, the loyal son who was willing to be sacrificed; Rebekah, a courageous woman with a wonderful attitude of service— how extensive were their shortcomings in God's eyes? And how much more fulfillment might they have known, had they done their best in their obedience to the Lord?

Jacob and Esau were the last of the once–promising nuclear family. With problems of their own—many of their own creation—they still managed to part company peacefully to take different paths through life. Esau moved back to the hill country of Seir. Never again would the brothers or their kin bond as closely or as kindly as they did for that short time in Canaan. (In fact, some of Esau's children would become mortal enemies of the Israelites. Esau himself became the father of the Edomites, and his son Amalek, the father of the Amelekites.) In the near and distant future, descendants of both brothers would live in close proximity—but certainly not in peace.

Chapter 14

Joseph and Judah

Profiles of Prophecy

The book of Genesis next shifts away from Jacob to center on his son Joseph, one of my favorite characters. Once he grew up (and what a process of maturation!), Joseph was the right man, in the right place, for the right time to save Israel and preserve God's covenant. Unfortunately, though, he began life as a pampered child, better loved than even his younger brother, Benjamin.

Just imagine, though, what it must have been like with thirteen children in the family, some old enough to be more like parents than siblings. Imagine the noise and energy level in a home where the insanity surrounding the teen years is repeated so many times. As a parent, it would not have been an easy task to treat each child fairly, making sure each had the time, affirmation, and attention necessary to grow into independent, functional adults. Jacob showed his favoritism by giving Joseph a special garment, a one–of–a–kind coat. When the rest of the boys were wearing off–the–rack, feedbag brown, Joseph was wearing the whole spectrum of color—and his brothers hated him for it: "Now Israel [Jacob] loved Joseph more than any of his other sons, because he had been born to him in his old age; and he made a richly ornamented robe for him. When his brothers saw that their father loved him more than any of them, they hated him and could not speak a kind word to him" (37:3–4).

In addition to being spoiled by his father, Joseph also served as a snitch for him, spying on his older brothers and reporting only their bad behavior and mistakes. The more Joseph snitched, the more Jacob favored him and the more the others resented the situation. Joseph managed in the process, albeit unwittingly, to unite his brothers against one common enemy—himself. Even Dan and Naphtali could bond with Reuben in a common cause despite his flagrant offense to their portion of the family.

As if he was not already the target of his brothers' animosity, Joseph would continuously announce having prophetic dreams, in which the brothers were cast as villains and Joseph, the hero! One dream in particular caused them to despise him all the more. Joseph boasted, "Listen to this dream I had: We were binding sheaves of grain out in the field when suddenly my sheaf rose and stood upright, while your sheaves gathered around mine and bowed down to it" (37:6–7).

The brothers were enraged. "Do you intend to reign over us? Will you actually rule us?" (37:8). They seethed with jealousy.

Joseph then had another dream, which he again eagerly told to his brothers and also his father: "This time the sun and moon and eleven stars were bowing down to me" (37:9). Even Jacob was a little irked with Joseph by this point but did not make a big deal of it (see 37:10–11).

Jacob had reached his golden years and had moved to the executive suite, while his sons were left with the grunt work. With the older boys in charge of the sheep, Joseph was promoted to the middle management position of "snitch." So when the brothers stayed near Shechem with the flocks, Jacob sent Joseph to check out the situation and report on how things were going. Since his sons were "character clones" of their father, Jacob naturally assumed they were either lazy or up to no good (see 37:12–14).

What was the mood like in Shechem when the locals knew the Jacob Gang was lurking? If they had heard of "the Dinah retaliation," they would have been understandibly terrified. When Joseph arrived in Shechem, where he thought his brothers would be, he could not find them. He asked a man about their whereabouts, and the man directed him (hastily, no doubt) toward Dothan (see 37:15–17). The narrative succinctly states that when the brothers saw Joseph coming, "before he reached them, they plotted to kill him" (37:18). They had spotted Joseph from far away—how could they miss the little prince strutting down the path, wearing his funky coat with all the bright colors?

From what we know of the brothers, they may have been near the flocks but were probably not paying a great deal of attention to them. Maybe they were playing cards or roasting mutton over a campfire. Tending sheep was boring work, but plotting to kill should not be among the activities used to pass the time. "'Here comes that dreamer!' they said to each other" (37:19). (What do you bet they had other pet names for brother Joseph not repeatable in polite company?) "Come now, [Let's fix this little fink once and for all!] let's kill him and throw him into one of these cisterns and say that a ferocious animal devoured him. Then we'll see what comes of his dreams" (37:20). They wanted to chuck Joseph down a dry well—not to scare him or teach him a lesson, but to leave him there to die. And they loathed him to the point that they were willing to give perjured testimony about his disappearance.

When Reuben heard the plot to kill Joseph, to his limited credit, he tried to convince the others not kill him. "Let's not take his life. . . . Don't shed any blood. Throw him into this cistern here in the desert, but don't lay a hand on him" (37:21–22). Apparently Reuben planned to pull Joseph out of the dry well later and take him home. Did Reuben have a sudden attack of moral values, or did he just want to rehabilitate his reputation as one who might still be the best choice as heir?

Plotting how to kill Joseph must have been a popular topic of conversation around the campfire because the details of the conspiracy fell into place in short order. As Joseph approached, he should have sensed that something was amiss. His brothers, usually a surly lot, grew quite animated—talking, smiling, and gesturing at Joseph. When he walked into camp oblivious to the danger, the brothers grabbed him, roughed him up, stripped off his special robe, belted him a few more times for good measure, and tossed him down the dry well (see 37:23–24).

Relieved to have rid themselves of their major irritant, the brothers then sat down to eat, paying no attention to Joseph's moans and cries for help. Reuben, perhaps looking for a way to get Joseph out of the well, was not there with them. As they ate, the boys spied a caravan of Ishmaelites coming from Gilead with camels loaded with spices, balm, and myrrh on their way to Egypt. These were descendants of their grandfather's half–brother Ishmael, not held in high esteem.

Judah shrewdly recognized an opportunity to solve their "problem" without actually committing murder: "What will we gain if we kill our brother and cover up his blood? . . . Let's sell him to the Ishmaelites and not lay our hands on him; after all, he is our brother, our own flesh and blood" (37:26–27). I seriously doubt if Judah or the others had any scruples about killing Joseph, flesh and blood or not, but they all agreed it was a superb idea. When the caravan came by, they fished Joseph out of the dry well, haggled a fair price for a new slave in good condition—just slightly bruised—and banked twenty shekels of silver (see 37:28). They had learned well from their father Jacob—they could beat one of their own and still find a way to make a profit.

By the time Reuben returned to the cistern, all he found was Joseph's trademark robe, lots of hoofprints from the caravan, and the smug smiles of the brothers as they counted out their shares of silver. "The boy isn't there! Where can I turn now?" Reuben frantically asked, perhaps more afraid for himself and his status than for Joseph (37:30).

The brothers had to stick together and come up with a story that would creatively "explain" to Jacob what had happened to Joseph. So they shredded his robe and smeared it with goat's blood to make it look like Joseph had been torn to bits by a wild animal. (Today, any rookie forensic technician would have easily determined that the blood was not human. But in that era, blood was blood, especially to a distraught parent.) The brothers returned home and presented the blood–soaked garment to Jacob: "We found this. Examine it to see whether it is your son's robe" (37:32).

As soon as Jacob saw the coat, he recognized it and jumped to the desired conclusion with no additional explanation needed: "It is my son's robe! Some ferocious animal has devoured him. Joseph has surely been torn to pieces" (37:33). After that, nothing could be said or done to bring Jacob any comfort despite family visitations, which included the ten co–conspirators. Despairing of life, Jacob sobbed and wailed,

"In mourning will I go down to the grave to my son" (37:35).

Did the brothers feel any regret for the anguish they caused their father, or did they justify their actions by thinking that Joseph had it coming? Perhaps they even had to stifle a chuckle when they spoke of Joseph. But they all stuck to the story, and life went on as usual. Benjamin stayed at home to keep his father company, and the others did not seem to mind. Benjamin was young enough not to pose a threat. At least he did not have those strange dreams.

Joseph was sold to an Egyptian named Potiphar, the captain of the guard, one of Pharaoh's top cabinet officials (see 37:36). In Egypt, Joseph's life was to take other abrupt turns—sometimes for the better, sometimes for the worse, but always for the Lord's purpose.

Surely Jacob must have felt that life had spun way out of control. His favorite wife—dead; favorite son—dead, or so he thought; first born son—having an affair with one of his wives. Where would it end?

Judah's Family Line

The saga continues next with the life of Jacob's third son, Judah, who decided to break away from parental and sibling influences and strike out on his own: "At that time, Judah left his brothers and went down to stay with a man of Adullam named Hirah. There Judah met the daughter of a Canaanite man" (38:1–2). When Judah went looking for a wife, he should have visited a well at water–drawing time. That plan had always seemed to work. But shunning the advice of previous generations not to marry foreigners, Judah married this Canaanite woman, who conceived and gave him a son named Er (see 38:3). (I wonder if that name was taken from Judah's hesitant response to the question, "Honey, what shall we name the boy?")

How long any of this took is not reported, but Judah must have had a whirlwind courtship and wedding. Apparently, after hearing the story of his father's fourteen–year servitude for the wife he wanted, Judah wasn't going to wait. Later, Judah and his wife had another son, Onan, and another son after that named Shelah.

Ironically, the city of Adullam lay near what would one day be the city of Jerusalem, in the region that would become the parcel of territory allocated to the descendants of Judah. Although he thought he was getting away from home, Judah was, in fact, venturing into the land that would be his tribe's inheritance hundreds of years later.

The Bible then demonstrates in Judah's tale how time can be compressed in narration. Although his family line was essential to the prophecy of the Messiah, Judah is not a primary character in Genesis. So no sooner was Er born than Judah found him a wife! The young lady's name was Tamar. And no sooner did Er have a wife than the Lord found him to be wicked and put him to death (see 38:6–7).

Normally it is not the Lord's practice to remove those who have displeased Him. If God went around killing everyone who was wicked, disobedient or rebellious, there would be no need to chronicle Genesis or any other book of the Bible because no one would be left to read it! Since the days of Adam and Eve, we have had a hard time interacting honestly with God—or even with our own families. But Er must have really been a piece of work for the Lord to cancel his membership in the human race.

Whatever the reason, Er died young and without an heir. According to the law of that time, Onan was required to marry Er's widow to make sure the estate of the deceased remained in the family. This was called a levirate marriage, from the Latin translation of the Hebrew *levir*, meaning "brother–in–law," and it ensured that the deceased's inheritance rights, as well as the young widow's, were protected. (Ruth 4:5–6 outlines the levirate principle of the kinsman-redeemer, where a family member married a widow to maintain the line.) It was Onan's duty to the family, therefore, to have a child with his sister–in–law to perpetuate his dead brother's inheritance. But Onan did not wish to father a child that would never be considered his own, despite his biological parenthood. He failed to "perform his duty," and for this he incurred the wrath of God. So the Lord cancelled Onan's membership, too (see 38:8–10).

Poor Tamar remained a widow and alone. Judah then offered his solution to the situation—she was to go home to her own father's house and live there as a widow until Judah's son Shelah grew old enough to marry. Tamar had to think that was a bit of a stretch—to wait so long for a husband, not knowing how old the lad was. And would he fit the family pattern and die like his two brothers? Nevertheless, Tamar obediently returned to her father's house. Judah, however, never intended for Shelah to marry her.

Scripture then says, "After a long time Judah's wife, the daughter of Shua, died. When Judah had recovered from his grief, he went up to Timnah, to the men who were shearing his sheep, and his friend Hirah the Adullamite went with him" (38:12). Hirah had been one of the first to befriend Judah when he left home and began his quest for a bride.

When Tamar heard that her father–in–law was coming to Timnah—news travels fast with some families—she devised a plan to remind Judah of his unfulfilled pledge. Shelah had grown and was eligible for marriage, and Tamar was going to hold Judah to his promise. Changing out of her traditional, dark widow's clothes into something more colorful, she covered her face with a veil and took a seat by the entrance to the town of Enaim, on the road to Timnah, where the pagan shrine prostitutes sat waiting for "worshippers" to hire their services as an offering to the Canaanite deities. A woman seated there in widow's clothes and without a veil would have been out of place (see 38:13–14).

When Judah came along, he saw Tamar and thought she was a prostitute. Over the years Jacob must not have given his sons a solid foundation in the principles of true worship, for as soon as Judah saw her, he figured, *"When in Rome . . . ,"* and recruited her sexual favors.

"Come now, let me sleep with you," Judah said, not realizing she was his daughter–in–law.

"And what will you give me to sleep with you?" Tamar asked, negotiating her price.

Judah offered, "I'll send you a young goat from my flock." I guess that was generous in those days.

Tamar asked her customer to leave a pledge, collateral if you will, to make sure that once he left, his promise would not be forgotten. No one carried goats in their wallet. And besides, his promises had been worthless to her so far.

As a man of reasonably honorable intentions, Judah agreed. He left her with his seal, its cord, and his staff—all three items easily identifiable and valuable enough to come back for. The seal (a personalized, engraved cylinder) identified documents, and when rolled on a clay writing tablet, its mark equated to a formal signature. The fancy decorated cord allowed the owner to wear the seal around the neck for safe keeping and convenience. Anyone possessing the seal could represent Judah in financial transactions. After negotiating the demands, Judah had sex with Tamar—and she became pregnant (see 38:15–18).

Judah went on his way, and Tamar changed back into her widow's clothes. As agreed, Judah sent the goat to her by way of his friend Hirah. But when Hirah arrived, with goat, back at the gate to the town, there was no woman. He asked the local men, "Where is the shrine prostitute who was beside the road at Enaim?" (38:21). They gave him a quizzical look as if to question his eyesight or his sanity, claiming that there had not been a prostitute around there. Judah's friend then returned and explained that he could not find the woman in question.

Judah, having made the attempt to pay, was probably quick to say, "Let her keep what she has, or we will become a laughingstock" (38:23). I like the way he chose to use "we" instead of "I" when referring to the indignity of running around asking about imaginary prostitutes. He may even have been quite pleased with himself, for he kept the goat, could make another seal, and had a pleasant time with the young lady—that cost him nothing. Old Jacob would have been proud.

About three months later, Judah heard that daughter–in–law Tamar, who was supposed to be in mourning and celibate, was in fact pregnant. This, of course, was a capital offense. Furious over this insult to his family's dignity, Judah demanded that she be burned to death (see 38:24). Due process was not a consideration in those days, and the accused could not confront their accuser or present evidence at trial. So as the angry mob stormed the house to bring Tamar out by force, she sent word to Judah along with his three belongings, stating matter of factly: "I am pregnant by the man who owns these" (38:25).

When Judah saw his personal items, he immediately knew who was at fault. He said, "She is more righteous than I, since I wouldn't give her to my son Shelah" (38:26). Scripture does not specify what then took place, but I imagine that he was compelled to make a public apology. For once, Judah did the right thing in telling the truth—a commodity often in short supply among his ancestors and extended family. The mob, of course, let Tamar go.

"When the time came for her [Tamar] to give birth, there were twin boys in her womb" (38:27). The Abraham/Isaac/Jacob family had not fared well with twins before, but during labor, one of the babies put his hand through Tamar's birth canal. The midwife tied a red string around the tiny hand, making the comment, "This one came out first." But the child drew back his hand, and his brother was born first. He was greeted with, "So this is how you have broken out!" and he was named Perez, meaning "breaking out." The brother with the scarlet thread on his wrist was named Zerah, meaning "scarlet" (see 38:28–30).

Judah's descendants would carry on the family line all the way to the Messiah—a long line of misfits, ne'er–do–wells, and dysfunctionals. Of course, Jesus was not one Himself, but His own family lineage extended way back beyond Mary and Joseph. The family line of Perez would continue through successive generations to King David (see Ruth 4:18–22) and on through, in the fullness of time, to Jesus Christ—the Redeemer for all sinful, dysfunctional mankind, including His relatives.

Chapter 15

Joseph

From Slave to Savior

While Judah fathered twins, the rest of the brothers probably tended sheep back in Canaan and kept a lid on their secret, as they tried their best to forget about Joseph. Too bad they had broken the old man's heart in that process. Jacob pined for Joseph each day, wondering what he might have done differently to save his son.

Meanwhile, Joseph—still very much alive—worked as a slave in Potiphar's household. But the Lord continued to watch over Joseph, allowing everything he did for his new master to flourish. Before long, Potiphar took notice of the admirable qualities of this young man and saw that success followed him, so he made Joseph his chief attendant. Potiphar placed his Hebrew captive "in charge of his household, and he entrusted to his care everything he owned" (39:4). In fact, bringing prosperity to Joseph's Egyptian masters was to begin the fulfillment of the Abrahamic promise.

"What's That You Say, Mrs. Potiphar?"

Joseph was given the run of the estate and was trusted to handle everything—everything except Mrs. Potiphar, the one variable in this seemingly ideal situation. Potiphar's wife soon "took notice" of Joseph. Impressed with his striking good looks and seeking a relationship decidedly more carnal than platonic, she propositioned him with what sounded more like an order than a seduction. "Come to bed with me!"

(39:7). If this statement were made today, it certainly would constitute sexual harassment in the workplace. But Joseph was a slave, not an employee, with no rights to disobey an order from the master or mistress who owned him. To his credit, Joseph dealt with the issue as diplomatically as possible—for what appears to have been a considerable period of time. He had made up his mind not to give in to Mrs. Potiphar's repeated sexual advances and rebuffed her appeals, saying, "My master has withheld nothing from me except you, because you are his wife. How then could I do such a wicked thing and sin against God?" (39:9). Joseph had learned something greater than anything his father Jacob could have taught him—honesty. Would Jacob have been as trustworthy and loyal in similar circumstances?

The Bible is filled with accounts of those who allowed unexpected temptation into their hearts, almost welcoming sin and lust to enter. Remember Samson, who fell hard for Delilah while she ensnared him and gave him the world's most infamous haircut? Then consider King David, who should have gone back to bed when he saw Bathsheba bathing on the rooftop below. Instead, sexual temptation nearly ruined his leadership. But Joseph knew the Lord was involved in his life, attesting to all the ways he had been rescued from harm. He was running the estate of one of the most influential men in all of Egypt, rather than building tombs and monuments for the Pharaohs, where one's life expectancy was often counted in days, not years.

We do not know much about Mrs. Potiphar, not even her first name. She may have resembled the spoiled, pampered rich characters from daytime television soap operas—the ones with nothing more to do than hatch plots and change from one designer outfit to another. Perhaps she had too much time and too much money for her own good. Was she left alone too often, as Potiphar, captain of the guard, dealt with threats to national security that required much of his attention?

Day after day Potiphar's wife tried to wear down Joseph's resolve with seductive words and passionate entreaties. But Joseph would have none of it. He tried to make sure he was never alone with her, avoiding even the slightest hint of impropriety. But one day, all the other servants were occupied elsewhere, leaving Joseph alone with Mrs. Potiphar, dressed in the flimsiest negligee she could find from

"Nefertiti's Secret" catalog. Joseph knew that she was the predator and he was the prey. Trapped, he turned to run, and she grabbed him by the cloak, ordering him again to "come to bed." Joseph did a quick inside spin, worthy of NBA standards, and slid out of his cloak, leaving her holding it. He made his escape out of the house, running as fast as he could (see 39:10–12).

Frustrated beyond reason, Mrs. Potiphar shouted for her servants. Then lying to avoid scandal, she said to them: "This Hebrew has been brought to us to make sport of us! He came in here to sleep with me, but I screamed. When he heard me scream for help, he left his cloak beside me and ran out of the house" (39:14–15). She kept the cloak handy until Potiphar returned home that evening. As he walked through the door, she confronted him with the same fabricated story of the alleged assault, but added a dose of guilt by referring to "the slave *you* brought us" and remarked "how *your* slave treated me"—as if Potiphar was somehow responsible for the attack. She also reiterated the fact that Joseph, "that Hebrew slave," had tried to capitalize on her Egyptian husband's cultural prejudice (see 39:16–19).

When Potiphar heard the lurid details, he was furious and ordered Joseph's arrest. With no hearing, no reading of his rights, and no attorney, Joseph was jailed "where the king's prisoners were confined" (39:20). A commonly held belief of Bible scholars is that this prison was a less secure facility, where treatment of prisoners may have been less harsh than in prisons reserved for more violent felons. Joseph found himself in a dire state, regardless of the three–star rated institution, and yet Scripture says that

> while Joseph was there in the prison, the Lord was with him; He showed him kindness and granted him favor in the eyes of the prison warden. So the warden put Joseph in charge of all those held in the prison, and he was made responsible for all that was done there. The warden paid no attention to anything under Joseph's care, because the Lord was with Joseph and gave him success in whatever he did (39:20–23).

Once again, the Lord watched over Joseph so that even in the slammer, the warden knew that Joseph could be trusted with any task.

The Baker, the Cupbearer, and the Dream Maker

At some point during his incarceration, Joseph received two new inmates to care for—the king's baker and his cupbearer. The cupbearer never left the king's side, much like a combination bodyguard, food taster, and personal gofer. Both had done something to offend their master, so Pharaoh had locked them "in the house of the captain of the guard, in the same prison where Joseph was confined" (40:3). Since Pharaoh had placed these two in the custody of the captain of the guard, this same captain—possibly Potiphar—had assigned them to Joseph. Despite the alleged assault, Potiphar apparently trusted Joseph—perhaps more than he trusted his wife.

Once Potiphar's wrath had subsided, he might have realized he had been duped. And how often? Had Mrs. Potiphar conducted many affairs behind her husband's back? Had Potiphar deluded himself for years by refusing to believe all the rumors of her promiscuity? We will never know. Potiphar trusted Joseph and finally accepted the heartbreak of his wife's infidelity, knowing Joseph could not possibly be guilty of the attempted sexual assault. But by then, there was little that he could do except to put Joseph in confinement, where he would not be harmed and could continue to use his organizational gifts as before.

Furthermore, Pharaoh was spared a political nightmare involving one of his most trusted officials. If Potiphar had Joseph immediately jailed, there would be no publicity, no trial, no 'round–the–clock news coverage. If he let him go, there would be chaos. Mrs. Potiphar would appear on all the talk shows to publicize her new book, *The Hebrew Kid Did It*. We can also presume that, by having Joseph immediately jailed, Potiphar became God's instrument of protection for him and, therefore, all of Israel.

Under Joseph's watch, the cupbearer and the baker remained in custody "for some time." One morning Joseph noticed that they both appeared visibly upset by something. When he asked them about it, they replied, "We both had dreams . . . but there is no one to interpret them" (40:8). In the days before Freud's work on dream interpretation, people viewed dreams as metaphysical revelations of the future. When a vivid yet confusing dream could not be interpreted, it was most unsettling. But these two inmates were assigned to the care of the dreammeister himself. An accident? I don't think so.

Joseph encouraged them to tell him their dreams, so the cupbearer went first: "In my dream I saw a vine in front of me, and on the vine were three branches. As soon as it budded, it blossomed, and its clusters ripened into grapes. Pharaoh's cup was in my hand, and I took the grapes, squeezed them into Pharaoh's cup and put the cup in his hand" (40:9–11).

Then Joseph gave him the following interpretation: "The three branches are three days. Within three days Pharaoh will lift up your head and restore you to your position, and you will put Pharaoh's cup in his hand, just as you used to do when you were his cupbearer" (40:12–13). Giving the interpretation freely, Joseph did make one request—"When all goes well with you, remember me and show me kindness; mention me to Pharaoh and get me out of this prison" (40:14).

The baker, having heard the cupbearer's good news, also decided to relate his dream to Joseph: "On my head were three baskets of bread. In the top basket were all kinds of baked goods for Pharaoh, but the birds were eating them out of the basket on my head" (40:16–17).

I wonder if Joseph's body language gave away the fact that his interpretation was not encouraging at all: "This is what it means. . . . The three baskets are three days. Within three days Pharaoh will lift off your head and hang you on a tree. And the birds will eat away your flesh" (40:18–19).

It is one thing to interpret a dream; it is quite another to predict the future and have those events happen. That is the true test of a prophet. Three days following Joseph's interpretation of the dreams, Pharaoh celebrated his birthday with a feast for all his leaders and top political people. During the gala, the Egyptian king "lifted up the heads of the chief cupbearer and the chief baker," which means he had them formally stand before him face-to-face (see 40:20). Feeling confident that the cupbearer had learned his lesson, Pharaoh restored him to his previous position. But at the same time, the baker, who must have done something really bad, was taken out and hanged. And as his body hung there, twisting in the breeze, as a warning to others who would be derelict in their duty, the prophecies came true—exactly as Joseph had said (see 40:21–22). The cupbearer, though, forgot to mention Joseph's plight to the king.

Dreams, the very thing that got Joseph into trouble in the first place, would also be his ticket out of jail—eventually. His interpretations of them would also provide opportunities never available back in Canaan. Joseph's most notable character trait, however, was that through all of his misfortunes he never complained or schemed his way to a better deal like his father Jacob or his grandfather Isaac. Perhaps for the first time in several generations, a member of the dysfunctional Genesis family showed compelling evidence of spiritual maturity.

Joseph's Ticket Out of the Slammer

Joseph remained in prison for another two years until, like the cupbearer and baker before him, Pharaoh was troubled by dreams. Were they prompted by something he ate before going to bed? Or were they from the stress of managing the Egyptian empire? Whatever the cause, the king felt they were not just sleep disturbances but revelations of the future. In the first dream, Pharaoh stood by the edge of the Nile River

> when out of the river there came up seven cows, sleek and fat, and they grazed among the reeds. After them, seven other cows, ugly and gaunt, came up out of the Nile and stood beside those on the riverbank. And the cows that were ugly and gaunt ate up the seven sleek, fat cows (41:2–4).

Then he awoke with a start. (The sight of anorexic, cannibalistic cows eating their fellow bovines must have jarred him awake. It would me. But that dream sure beats the one about showing up at school in your pajamas. You have had that one before, right?) When he fell asleep again, he had a second dream:

> Seven heads of grain, healthy and good, were growing on a single stalk. After them, seven other heads of grain sprouted—thin and scorched by the east wind. The thin heads of grain swallowed up the seven healthy, full heads (41:5–7).

When Pharaoh awoke, more terrified than even before, he knew he was just dreaming; yet the images stayed fresh in his mind and bothered him all through the night. He sensed that his dreams portended something significant, perhaps even urgent, but he did not have a clue as to what it was. He sent for "all the magicians and wise men of Egypt" and recounted his dreams to see if they could decipher them, but they were as baffled as he was (see 41:8).

Finally remembering his long overdue promise in one of those "oops" moments we all have at times, the chief cupbearer told Pharaoh, "Today I am reminded of my shortcomings. . . . A young Hebrew was there [in prison] with us, a servant of the captain of the guard. We told him our dreams, and he interpreted them for us, . . . And things turned out exactly as he interpreted them to us" (41:9–13).

The king immediately sent for Joseph, who was rushed from the prison, given a new set of clothes, and made presentable. What did Joseph think would happen to him? *Am I being set free, or is Pharaoh going to sentence me for the "assault" on Potiphar's wife that never happened?* But Pharaoh had a different agenda. When Joseph appeared before him, the king said, "I have heard it said of you that when you hear a dream you can interpret it" (41:15). This was the opportunity Joseph had prayed for. All he had to do was parlay any interpretation into an escape from Egypt!

Instead, Joseph spoke the truth with a refreshing mix of confidence and humility. With great poise, given his predicament, he replied, "I cannot do it, . . . but God will give Pharaoh the answer he desires" (41:16). So Pharaoh recounted the dreams in detail as Joseph listened patiently before making any comment. Finally Joseph said,

> The dreams of Pharaoh are one and the same. God has revealed to Pharaoh what He is about to do. The seven good cows are seven years, and the seven good heads of grain are seven years; it is one and the same dream. The seven lean, ugly cows that came up afterward are seven years, and so are the seven worthless heads of grain scorched by the east wind: They are seven years of famine. . . . Seven years of great abundance are coming throughout the land of Egypt, but seven years of famine

will follow them. Then all the abundance in Egypt will be forgotten, and the famine will ravage the land. The abundance in the land will not be remembered, because the famine that follows it will be so severe (41:25–27,29–31).

Not wanting to leave his interpretation out there with no solution to the impending disaster, Joseph advised Pharaoh to

look for a discerning and wise man and put him in charge of the land of Egypt. Let Pharaoh appoint commissioners over the land to take a fifth of the harvest of Egypt during the seven years of abundance. They should collect all the food of these good years that are coming and store up the grain under the authority of Pharaoh, to be kept in the cities for food. This food should be held in reserve for the country, to be used during the seven years of famine that will come upon Egypt, so that the country may not be ruined by the famine (41:33–36).

It seems short–sighted for Egyptians not to have considered the prudence of stockpiling food in times of plenty to hold them through times of famine. But valuing good advice when he heard it—and he did not hear it often from the usual coterie of yes–men and favor–seekers— Pharaoh took Joseph's idea and ran with it. After contemplating the qualities of the position needed, he stood, pointed to Joseph and proclaimed to the entire court: "Since God has made all this known to you, there is no one so discerning and wise as you. You shall be in charge of my palace, and all my people are to submit to your orders. Only with respect to the throne will I be greater than you. . . . I hereby put you in charge of the whole land of Egypt" (41:39–41). Pharaoh took off his signet ring, used to sign laws and official documents, and placed it on Joseph's finger.

Joseph was dressed in fine linen and given a gold chain to wear around his neck, a symbol of high office. He rode in a chariot as Pharaoh's second in command, and men shouted "Make way!" as he passed. Had he been a vindictive person, Joseph might have made an official visit to Potiphar's house to settle an old score.

Pharaoh had personally commissioned Joseph to take the necessary steps to save the people from the coming famine, giving him nearly unlimited authority to establish and enforce policy—not too shabby for a thirty–year–old ex–con from Canaan. The last blessing that the king bestowed on Joseph was to give him a royal Egyptian name, Zaphenath–Paneah, and a wife, Asenath (see 41:44–46).

During the first seven fat–cow, full–heads–of–grain years, the land produced such abundance that Joseph amassed great quantities of food to store in the royal granaries. As he traveled throughout the land of Egypt, he kept the stored produce close to where it was grown so the people would see the results of their efforts. Joseph did his job so well that eventually the quantities of grain grew so vast that they could not be counted (see 41:47–49).

Before the onset of the global food crisis, Joseph and Asenath had two sons. The first was named Manasseh, possibly derived from the Hebrew for "forget" because "God has made me forget all my trouble and all my father's household" (41:51). The second was named Ephraim, meaning "twice fruitful," "because God has made me fruitful in the land of my suffering" (41:52). In prosperity, as well as suffering, Joseph did not fail to remember that the Lord, his protector, works according to His divine plan.

Chapter 16

The Sons of Jacob

My Brother, the Governor

Predicted with the accuracy of a Swiss watch, "the seven years of abundance in Egypt came to an end, and the seven years of famine began, just as Joseph had said" (41:53–54). Each day brought reports of crop failures, drought, record heat, and pest infestation—the makings of a first–class food catastrophe. All that was missing was mad–cow and foot and mouth disease.

Now I don't think that one day people ate, and the next they starved. But I do imagine that each trip to the grocery store rapidly showed fewer and fewer things on the shelves. First the fresh produce, then the meat. With prime cuts gone, people were glad to get any part of the animal. Within a few months, cans of beets, asparagus, and creamed corn became delicacies. Kids no longer refused to eat certain things; they eagerly devoured whatever was set before them.

When the famine finally spread across the country, Joseph opened up the government–run storehouses and sold the grain to the Egyptians (see 41:56). It did not take long for news to get out that Egypt had food, thanks to Joseph's mandatory conservation program. Soon "all the countries came to Egypt to buy grain from Joseph, because the famine was severe in all the world" (41:57).

Back in Canaan, Jacob had heard that there was food for sale in Egypt, and he prodded his sons, "Why do you just keep looking at each other? . . . I have heard that there is grain in Egypt. Go down there and buy some for us, so that we may live and not die" (42:1–2). So Joseph's brothers loaded their camels and mules with enough sacks to carry as much grain as they could buy. Never fully recovering from losing Joseph, however, Jacob kept Benjamin safe at home.

After the arduous journey from Canaan, the brothers arrived in Egypt at one of the storehouses. They took a number and waited their turn with the others. When their number was called, they respectfully bowed to the well-dressed official, hoping to make a good impression. That might have meant clamping a hand over Reuben's mouth to make sure he did not say something that might get them thrown out. They remembered Jacob's stern warning that failure was not an option, and they had no desire to go home empty–handed. The brothers may have disliked having to behave like peasants, but all agreed that humble pie tasted much better than no pie at all.

As it happened, the official doling out the grain was also governor of the land—and their brother Joseph. The brothers bowed low with their faces to the ground to avoid any eye contact that might be construed as inappropriate. They did not recognize Joseph, but he knew exactly who they were. Under the circumstances, Joseph pretended not to know them and, feeling a twinge of revenge perhaps, accused them of being spies. "Where do you come from?" he asked (see 42:6–7).

The brothers replied, "From the land of Canaan. . . . [We] have come to buy food. We are all the sons of one man. Your servants are honest men, not spies" (42:7,10–11). No doubt beginning to sweat more from the terror of the angry governor than from the Egyptian sun, they began to babble and tell all their family history. (We have all done that under pressure, trying to explain so much that we could take a parking ticket and end up nearly confessing to the Great Train Robbery.) "Your servants were twelve brothers, the sons of one man who lives in the land of Canaan. The youngest is now with our father, and one is no more" (42:13).

Wanting to ascertain if his older brothers had changed or were sorry for what they had done years earlier, Joseph tested them: "You will not leave this place unless your youngest brother comes here. Send one of your number to get your brother; the rest of you will be kept in prison, so that your words may be tested to see if you are telling the truth. If you are not, . . . you are spies!" (42:15–16). Just to get their undivided attention, he locked them all up for three days.

On the third day, Joseph brought them back in and said: "Do this and you will live. . . . Let one of your brothers stay here in prison, while the rest of you go and take grain back for your starving households. But you must bring your youngest brother to me, so that your words may be verified and that you may not die" (42:18–20). The brothers politely obeyed, but in trying to understand their plight, they discussed the matter among themselves and came to some interesting conclusions that acknowledged their past culpability.

They said to one another, "Surely we are being punished because of our brother. We saw how distressed he was when he pleaded with us for his life, but we would not listen; that's why this distress has come upon us." Then Reuben interjected, "Didn't I tell you not to sin against the boy? But you wouldn't listen! Now we must give an accounting for his blood" (42:21–22). The old adage "Be sure your sins will find you out" is indeed true, for the matter would never be over until they accepted responsibility for their role in what happened to Joseph.

Meanwhile, their brother the governor was hearing every word they said. They did not realize, of course, that Joseph could understand them even though he used an interpreter. Joseph was so moved by their admission of wrongdoing that he had to turn away to hide his tears.

Governor Joseph chose Simeon to hold as ransom and had him bound and taken away to complete the illusion of outrage—and to make sure they brought Benjamin back as ordered. What were the brothers thinking as they watched Simeon being carted away? *He is as good as dead, for there is no way our father will allow Benjamin to leave home, famine or not.* Then "Joseph gave orders to fill their bags with grain" (42:25). Glad to have accomplished at least one good thing from this otherwise disastrous trip, the remaining brothers loaded the pack animals and set off for home. What they did not know was that Joseph had also ordered their payments in silver to be placed back in their sacks.

When they stopped for the night, one brother opened his sack to get some feed for the animals, and there was the silver he had left in Egypt for payment! How would they have reacted in the old days when they were impetuous, greedy copies of their father? Any one of the brothers would have quietly pocketed the money without saying a word. Instead, God's influence had been working on all of them. Immediately admitting the truth to his brothers, the one said, "My silver has been returned." And in their new mindset, they asked themselves, *What is the Lord doing to us?* (see 42:27–28). I wonder if any of them got much sleep that night wondering how a simple shopping trip had turned into a complicated hostage situation.

When the brothers made it home—one brother short—they told Jacob how "the man who is lord over the land" questioned them about their family and then accused them of being spies. They explained how they were forced to leave Simeon as a hostage until they brought back Benjamin to prove their honesty. As the brothers emptied their sacks to show their father their one accomplishment—food to sustain the family—one by one they discovered that their payments had been returned (see 42:29–35).

Jacob reacted by saying, "You have deprived me of my children. Joseph is no more and Simeon is no more, and now you want to take Benjamin. Everything is against me!" (42:36). Jacob wasn't worried about Simeon because the focus was always on Jacob. Still as self–absorbed as he had always been, Jacob cast *himself* in the role of the victim—"You have deprived *me*; everything is against *me*." Being a victim isn't comfortable since it involves unfair treatment. But a victim does have the benefit of not having to take any responsibility either for the victimization or its correction.

As the eldest and still somewhat de facto leader of the brothers, in spite of his shabby record, Reuben tried to step in and comfort his father and do the right thing this time. He said to Jacob, "You may put both of my sons to death if I do not bring him [Benjamin] back to you. Entrust him to my care, and I will bring him back" (42:37). Trying to show his honest intentions and prove his reliability, Reuben offered his sons as sacrifices if he did not bring Simeon and Benjamin back safe.

But Jacob replied, "My son will not go down there with you; his brother is dead and he is the only one left. If harm comes to him on the journey you are taking, you will bring my gray head down to the grave in sorrow" (42:38). What could Reuben's or any of the brothers' reactions have been to this telling statement? Jacob took all they had done of late, in obedience and a truthfulness uncharacteristic of the Genesis family, and rejected it—and them with it.

Just as Jacob's parents, Isaac and Rebekah, had shown extreme favoritism to their sons, Jacob demonstrated how brutally dysfunctional this family trait could be. Jacob's parents had a problem with unfair favoritism and conditional love—Isaac loved Esau, not for Esau but for the meat he provided; Rebekah loved Jacob because she could keep him close and use that relationship to their mutual advantage. The brothers might have grown to accept not being Jacob's favorite, but it must have hurt not to be considered worthy of any concern at all.

Priorities of an Empty Stomach

Once the family had consumed all the grain that had been brought back from Egypt, and with the severe famine still ravaging the land, hunger began to influence Jacob far more than overly protective, biased parental care ever could. Simeon was still imprisoned, and no progress had been made toward meeting Joseph's demands. Knowing that Jacob would gladly sacrifice an older son to protect Benjamin, Simeon must have despaired of ever seeing freedom again. But with the returned threat of starvation as a real possibility, Jacob said to the boys, "Go back and buy us a little more food" (43:2).

Judah then reminded Jacob that they would not receive any more food or see Simeon again unless they returned to Egypt with Benjamin. Judah said, "If you will send our brother along with us, we will go down and buy food for you. But if you will not send him, we will not go down, because the man said to us, 'You will not see my face again unless your brother is with you'" (43:4–5).

"Why did you bring this trouble on me by telling the man you had another brother?" Jacob demanded. Using his own twisted logic, Jacob was the wounded party. If they were to starve, it was because they went and blabbed that there was another brother at home.

With more than a little exasperation the brothers confronted Jacob sternly, "The man questioned us closely about our family. 'Is your father still living?' he asked us. 'Do you have another brother?' We simply answered his questions. How were we to know he would say, 'Bring your brother down here?'" (43:7).

After more bickering and blaming from Jacob and his boys, Judah again took the initiative:

> Send the boy along with me and we will go at once, so that we and you and our children may live and not die. I myself will guarantee his safety; you can hold me personally responsible for him. If I do not bring him back to you and set him here before you, I will bear the blame before you all my life. As it is, if we had not delayed, we could have gone and returned twice (43:8–10).

By mentioning the delay, had Judah finally managed to convince Jacob of his own role in this deepening crisis? Did Judah's statement convey a more threatening message to his father? In other words, "If anything happens to Benjamin, blame me; but if anything happens to Simeon because you have acted so foolishly, blaming us where there was no blame, it will be on your head. Consider that, and make up your mind."

Jacob relented and gave his consent with a defeated "If it must be, then do this" (43:11). Thinking that gifts might work with the Egyptian official the way they had helped with Esau, he gave special instructions.

> Put some of the best products of the land in your bags and take them down to the man as a gift—a little balm and a little honey, some spices and myrrh, some pistachio nuts and almonds. Take double the amount of silver with you, for you must return the silver that was put back into the mouths of your sacks. Perhaps it was a mistake. Take your brother also and go back to the man at once (43:11–13).

Almost as an afterthought, Jacob invoked the Lord's blessing on the mess he had created by his delays and insecurities: "And may God Almighty grant you mercy before the man so that he will let your other brother and Benjamin come back with you. As for me, if I am bereaved, I am bereaved" (43:14). After Jacob prayed to protect Benjamin and "what's–his–name," he then fired one last guilt shot—"If I am to die a poor, broken–hearted, emotionally crushed, sorrowful, grieving old man because of You, Lord, then so be it." Jacob's blessing may have come belatedly, but it was completely in character.

Back to Egypt—To Rescue or Ruin

When the boys arrived back in Egypt with their gifts, double the amount in silver, and Benjamin, they went straight to Joseph to settle things as quickly as possible. When Joseph saw Benjamin, he said nothing to his brothers but ordered his steward to take the men to Joseph's quarters and prepare dinner for them all (see 43:15–16).

But the men were in no mood for a banquet with everything still unsettled. They were frightened and thought, "We were brought here because of the silver that was put back into our sacks the first time. He [Joseph] wants to attack us and overpower us and seize us as slaves and take our donkeys" (43:18). It is amazing how unforgiven sin can create a sense of paranoia. What they had done to Joseph was exactly the fate they thought would be theirs. Even in those ancient times they knew that what goes around, comes around. (Surprisingly, too, they appeared to hold their donkeys in higher regard than each other.)

Wanting to get out of Egypt as free men, they approached Joseph's steward at the entrance to the house and frantically recounted the story of how they had paid for the grain and then found the silver in their possession again. You can almost hear their quaking voices as they explained their situation (see 43:19–22). It may have been like the carefully memorized sales pitch that kids use when they sell candy door to door for a school project. You cannot interrupt the spiel to ask a question or they will have to begin again. Better to just let them blurt it out all at once.

The steward reassured the men that there was no problem—he had received the silver from his master and had returned it as he was told. Then he brought Simeon out to them unharmed (see 43:23). A collective sigh of relief must have filled the room! The brothers were given water to wash the dust off their feet and provided with fodder for their donkeys. When they were told they would dine with the Egyptian official, they began to prepare their gifts for him (see 43: 24–25).

In the old days they might have entertained the idea of keeping some of the gifts for themselves—to make up for their inconvenience. But instead, they would not keep so much as one pistachio nut, for this was a man worthy of their respect—he was shrewd, potentially deadly, and not one to suffer fools or deceivers.

When Joseph entered his house, the brothers bowed again with great solemnity and presented their gifts. I wonder if Joseph recalled with a smile his dream of long ago—the dream which his brothers took for arrogance (see 37:5–8). Now the dream had become reality, as the brothers, seeking food, bowed to the one who could help them.

After the brothers were finished with their speeches and presentations, Joseph put them at ease by exchanging pleasantries concerning the trip to Egypt and their lives in Canaan. When they seemed more relaxed, he asked, "How is your aged father you told me about? Is he still living?" (43:27).

"Your servant our father is still alive and well," the boys responded (43:28). This reference to Jacob as Joseph's servant made his second dream, in which even his father would bow to him, come to fruition (see 37:9–10).

But Joseph's real interest was Benjamin, the one with the DNA code closest to his own. As he spotted Benjamin in the crowd of siblings, he asked, "Is this your youngest brother, the one you told me about?" Joseph spoke tenderly to the boy, "God be gracious to you, my son" (43:29). He was so deeply affected by the sight of his little brother after so many years that Joseph had to retire to a private room where he broke down. Were these tears of joy at seeing how Benjamin had grown into a young man, or were they tears of regret for all the years spent apart from him?

After Joseph composed himself, since real men don't eat quiche or cry, he gave the order to serve dinner. What a lavish spread it must have been! Joseph, however, was served separately from the brothers. Although the boys were treated as honored guests, good Egyptians did not eat with the nomadic, rather backward Hebrew sheepherders—just as many generations later, good Jews had no dealings with Samaritans or Gentiles. It just wasn't done (see 43:31–32). Perhaps Joseph was delivering a subtle warning to his brothers not to get too comfortable. As dinner guests they were safe. But once out of the protection of his home, all bets were off.

Rather than simply inviting his brothers to sit down, Joseph had them seated by age—from eldest to youngest. No doubt that got their attention, since Joseph knew their birth order. They were astonished again during dinner when Benjamin received portions five times greater than anyone else's. But food was food and it was free, so the brothers feasted and drank their fill (see 43:33–34).

While the boys were occupied with dinner, Joseph gave instructions to his steward to load as much food as their donkeys could carry. And like the last time, the silver to pay for the grain went back in their packs as well. But Joseph also instructed the servant to hide Joseph's monogrammed, extremely valuable, easily identifiable ceremonial silver cup in Benjamin's gear (see 44:1–2). It was time to see if the boys had really changed.

Still feeling well fed and perhaps slightly hung–over from the ample food and drink, the brothers were sent home the next morning with their sacks filled with food. Once they were out of town, Joseph told his steward to form a posse and "Go after those men at once, and when you catch up with them, say to them, 'Why have you repaid good with evil? Isn't this the cup my master drinks from and also uses for divination? This is a wicked thing you have done'" (44:4–5). Joseph's charioteers quickly caught up with the brothers and arrested them for the alleged theft of the silver cup.

The brothers said, "Far be it from your servants to do anything like that! We even brought back to you from the land of Canaan the silver we found inside the mouths of our sacks. So why would we steal silver or gold from your master's house?" They were so confident of their innocence that they added, "If any of your servants is found to have it, he will die; and the rest of us will become my lord's slaves" (44:7–9). Eager to vindicate themselves, they readily submitted to the search beginning with the eldest, and, as expected, the cup was found in Benjamin's belongings. "At this, they tore their clothes"—a symbolic act of deep grief (44:13). Because clothes were hand–made from sheep to seamstress and not readily available, tearing something so valuable was a sign of great sorrow.

Knowing it was all some sort of horrific misunderstanding, the brothers returned to Joseph's house. When they saw him "they threw themselves to the ground before him" (44:14).

Judah spoke for them all. "What can we say to my lord? . . . How can we prove our innocence? God has uncovered your servants' guilt.

We are now my lord's slaves—we ourselves and the one who was found to have the cup" (44:16).

Joseph replied, "Far be it from me to do such a thing! Only the man who was found to have the cup will become my slave. The rest of you, go back to your father in peace" (44:17).

Judah acted as spokesman, not to talk their way out of their dilemma, but to set forth the effect Benjamin's arrest would have on their aged father. Judah recounted their previous conversations and Joseph's demand that they present the youngest brother. Never once did Judah shift any of the blame or accountability. At that point he had no information on Joseph and for all he knew he really was dead, and in fact mentions that there was another unaccounted for brother: "We have an aged father, and there is a young son born to him in his old age. His brother is dead, and he is the only one of his mother's sons left, and his father loves him" (44:20).

Eventually Judah gets to the place in the story where they have to take Benjamin back to Egypt after they convince the old man to allow him to leave. Judah continued, "Your servant my father said to us, 'You know that my wife bore me two sons. One of them went away from me, and I said, "He has surely been torn to pieces." And I have not seen him since. If you take this one from me too and harm comes to him, you will bring my gray head down to the grave in misery'" (44:27–29).

"Now then, please let your servant remain here as my lord's slave in place of the boy, and let the boy return with his brothers. How can I go back to my father if the boy is not with me? No! Do not let me see the misery that would come upon my father" (44:30–34).

Judah knew if they returned without Benjamin, the shock would kill Jacob—a chance he was not willing to take. Once he would have lied and schemed his way through, but now Judah could not treat his father with such cruelty, even if Dad never loved him or the rest as much as Joseph and Benjamin. Judah was more than wiling to take Benjamin's place, not knowing if that meant prison, slavery, or death.

Joseph was deeply impressed by Judah's impassioned plea, which was not for his own safety but for a higher loyalty to family and to doing the right thing regardless of the risk involved. When he could no longer hold back the need to reveal his identity, Joseph abruptly dismissed all the guards, servants, and attendants, leaving himself alone with his brothers, who still did not recognize him. He cried openly in front of them. Addressing them directly in Hebrew rather than in Egyptian through an interpreter, as he had done before, at last he said, "I am Joseph!" (45:3).

The boys were silent. Panic does that, for here was the brother they had long ago betrayed, holding their lives in the balance. Seeing their fear, Joseph prompted them, "'Come close to me.' When they had done so, he said, 'I am your brother Joseph, the one you sold into Egypt!'" (45:4). Why did Joseph urge them to come closer? Was there a word, a pet name, a family memory only they would recollect, which would convince them that the governor of Egypt was, in fact, their brother? This was probably the case, but with only vague childhood memories to go on, how could Joseph establish the truth of his claim to be their long–lost brother?

One possibility is that Joseph could have called them close to reveal the undeniable proof that he was of the family—of Abraham, Isaac, and Jacob. Remember that Joseph, unlike his fellow Egyptians, had been circumcised according to the tradition and command of God. "You can see for yourselves, . . . that it is really I who am speaking to you" (45:12).

Wanting to ease their fear and dissuade their guilt, Joseph also explained his destiny to them:

> Do not be distressed and do not be angry with yourselves
> for selling me here, because it was to save lives that God
> sent me ahead of you . . . to preserve for you a remnant on
> earth and to save your lives by a great deliverance. So
> then, it was not you who sent me here, but God (45:5–8).

What a reunion it must have been, as Joseph had a chance to tell of his adventures and the brothers shared their deepest regrets. He then gave them much more pleasant instructions than he had the last time:

> Hurry back to my father and say to him, "This is what
> your son Joseph says, 'God has made me lord of all Egypt.
> come down to me; don't delay. You shall live in the region
> of Goshen and be near me—you, your children and

grandchildren, your flocks and herds, and all you have. I will provide for you there, because five years of famine are still to come'" (45:9–11).

Joseph and Benjamin had some private time together, as they shared precious memories of their mother, Rachel. Lost time could never be reclaimed, but they would make good use of the opportunities that remained.

Even Pharaoh got into the spirit of the family reunion. He told Joseph to instruct his brothers to "bring your father and your families back to me. I will give you the best of the land of Egypt. . . . Take some carts from Egypt for your children and your wives, and get your father and come. Never mind about your belongings, because the best of all Egypt will be yours" (45:17–20).

Each of the brothers received a set of new clothes, but Benjamin received five sets of clothes and 300 shekels of silver. Joseph also sent his father an assortment of "the best things of Egypt," along with grain and bread and generous provisions for the journey (see 45:22–23).

When the brothers arrived back in Canaan, they ran to tell Jacob the wonderful news—"Joseph is not only alive but running Egypt's food supply. And we're moving to Egypt so we won't have to worry about starving to death!"

Of course, Jacob was stunned and speechless. He did not believe them. Since Joseph had been missing and presumed dead for so long, Jacob was going to require some convincing evidence to believe such a fantastic story. As they were explaining all that had transpired, Jacob "saw the carts Joseph had sent to carry him back [and] the spirit of their father Jacob revived" (45:27).

The wide–eyed Jacob replied, "I'm convinced! My son Joseph is still alive. I will go and see him before I die" (45:28).

Chapter 17

The Land of Goshen

Call the Movers!

Much like the classic commercial for Disney World, Jacob was bombarded with the announcement that changed his life: "Hey, Jacob! You have just discovered that your long–lost son Joseph is alive AND is the second most powerful man in Egypt. WHAT ARE YOU GOING TO DO NEXT?"

"We're going to Egypt!"

Not needing to pack any bags, Jacob hopped on a cart, and the whole family began the journey to Egypt. (The brothers must have felt as if they could walk the route blindfolded by now.) When they had traveled as far as Beersheba, Jacob offered sacrifices to the Lord. The sacrifices must have been accepted, for Scripture relates that during the night the Lord spoke to Jacob in a dream:

> I am God, the God of your father. . . . Do not be afraid to go down to Egypt, for I will make you into a great nation there. I will go down to Egypt with you, and I will surely bring you back again. And Joseph's own hand will close your eyes (46:3–4).

Once again, the Lord, who never forgets or breaks His covenants, promised that Jacob and all with him would be well cared for in Egypt, and that when he was old and near death, he would pass from this world to the next with Joseph at his side.

Riding in carts emblazoned with banners "Egypt or Bust," all of Jacob's offspring joined the wagon train bound for a new life in Goshen—seventy in all (see 46:7–27). Only seventy people—a long way from being "as numberless as the sands." They had not even totaled a tablespoon–sized scoop of beach yet. One item concerning Benjamin could be easily lost, however, in the cast of characters listed in Scripture. From previous references it would seem that Benjamin, as the last of Rachel's sons, was still a young man. But this record states that Benjamin had ten sons of his own by this time!

When the convoy arrived in Goshen, Joseph had his personal chauffeur get the chariot ready to meet Jacob. (This must have created quite a stir on the society pages of Egyptian papers, since a person of Joseph's stature would never ride off to meet anyone! People went to him!) When Joseph finally saw Jacob, "he threw his arms around his father and wept for a long time" (46:29).

The equally weepy–eyed Jacob said to Joseph, "Now I am ready to die, since I have seen for myself that you are still alive" (46:30). (I once saw a message with a similar sentiment on a T–shirt worn by a long–suffering New York Rangers hockey fan after the team had won the Stanley Cup for the first time in decades—"Now I can die happy.")

After the tears subsided, Joseph moved quickly to the pressing business of relocating all the relatives in Goshen. He coached them on what to say when they met Pharaoh. "When Pharaoh calls you in and asks, 'What is your occupation?' you should answer, 'Your servants have tended livestock from our boyhood on, just as our fathers did.' Then you will be allowed to settle in the region of Goshen, for all shepherds are detestable to the Egyptians" (46:33–34). At least in Goshen, they would be left alone and at peace.

Joseph selected five brothers to attend the royal interview. With great wisdom he probably had representation from each of the four mothers' sub–families to unite them in a common cause. The brothers answered Pharaoh exactly as Joseph had instructed.

Pharaoh said to Joseph, "Your father and your brothers have come to you, and the land of Egypt is before you; settle your father and your brothers in the best part of the land. Let them live in Goshen" (47:5–6).

For a dysfunctional family whose chief claim to fame was withstanding the consequences of being a gang of cheats, liars, swindlers, killers, adulterers, and ne'er do wells, the outcome looked pretty good. But when the Lord blesses a family that would become a nation, His grace overflows to cover even the vilest member.

Next, Joseph brought Jacob in to be presented before Pharaoh. The description in the Bible of their meeting is brief, yet I can imagine how eager Jacob might have been to offer the Egyptian king a father's sincere gratitude for caring for his boy and for trusting him with such great responsibilities. Likewise, Pharaoh was possibly most eager to gain a better understanding of how Joseph had become such a skilled administrator. If Jacob had taught these skills to Joseph, then perhaps those lessons could be taught to others. Sadly, this would have been wishful thinking on Pharaoh's part.

Pharaoh asked Jacob, "How old are you?" (47:8).

Scripture records Jacob's reply: "The years of my pilgrimage are a hundred and thirty. My years have been few and difficult, and they do not equal the years of the pilgrimage of my fathers" (47:9). The years were hard in large part because of his personal bent toward greed and ambition. Jacob failed to mention this, however.

Then Joseph settled his father and his brothers and their families on their new land and provided them with food according to the number of their children (see 47:11–12).

Pharaoh Plans Ahead

With the family back together, everyone was happy—although the entire region was still in the grip of famine. Joseph had collected all the money from those paying for grain and had brought the sums to Pharaoh's palace. With their money gone, starving citizens demanded food from the government reserves: "Give us food. Why should we die before your eyes? Our money is used up" (47:15).

Always thinking, Joseph responded, "I will sell you food in exchange for your livestock, since your money is gone" (47:16). So in came the horses, sheep, goats, cattle, and donkeys—and the people survived another year.

At the end of the year, the people came back to Joseph. "Since our money is gone and our livestock belongs to you, there is nothing left for our lord except our bodies and our land. . . . Buy us and our land in exchange for food, and we with our land will be in bondage to Pharaoh. Give us seed so that we may live" (47:18–19).

So in exchange for food, Joseph bought all the land for Pharaoh, who quickly owned everything in Egypt except for the priests' land because they received a stipend from Pharaoh and were never desperate enough to sell what they owned or offer themselves as indentured servants (see 47:20–22).

Joseph announced to the people, "Now that I have bought you and your land today for Pharaoh, here is seed for you so you can plant the ground. But when the crop comes in, give a fifth of it to Pharaoh. The other four–fifths you may keep as seed for the fields and as food for yourselves and your households and your children" (47:23–24). Joseph bought them not to make them slaves, but to rescue and redeem them while teaching them how to save for the future. And the people were grateful to him for saving their lives (see 47:25).

With that announcement, Joseph established a new law. One–fifth of all produce belonged to Pharaoh so there would always be adequate food reserves in case of emergencies (see 47:26).

As long as everyone was poor—each one as miserable as the next—things were fine. But over time, lingering resentment of the Hebrews for obtaining property and livestock at the expense of their Egyptian neighbors would eventually result in enslavement. Until then, the Hebrews settled in Goshen, acquiring property and remaining free to tend to their flocks and herds. As had been the case before with Jacob and Laban, harmony met with prosperity.

Jacob's Burial Request and Special Blessing

According to Scripture, Jacob lived seventeen years in Egypt and reached the fine old age of 147. When he knew his time remaining was short, Jacob chose to pass along the paternal legacy to Joseph—not the eldest, but the one who had saved the family from death.

Jacob said, "Promise that you will show me kindness and faithfulness. Do not bury me in Egypt, but when I rest with my fathers, carry me out of Egypt and bury me where they are buried" (47:29–30). After Joseph swore to take care of that last detail, Jacob "worshiped as he leaned on the top of his staff" (47:31). Perhaps the old guy was just strong enough to hold himself up by leaning on his shepherd's crook. For that moment, he wanted to look Joseph in the eye as he made his important request. He still had his pride, and the years had not diminished that trait one bit. Joseph could have arranged for a funeral fit for a king, but all Jacob wanted was to go home, even if he was not alive to enjoy the trip.

Some time later, Joseph received the news that Jacob was ill. He went to see his father and brought his two sons, Manasseh and Ephraim. Just knowing that Joseph had come was a tonic to the old man. He rallied what strength he had to sit up in bed and greet his son. Jacob reminded Joseph of all the Lord's promises concerning the future of their family (see 48:4). Although Joseph looked, sounded, and dressed Egyptian, he was part of the covenant family of Israel, sharing the benefits of God's inheritance equally with all the other descendants.

Since there was nothing Jacob could do for Joseph financially to show his gratitude, Jacob chose to grant special recognition to his two Egyptian–born grandsons to connect them to their Hebrew heritage:

> Now then, your two sons born to you in Egypt before I came to you here will be reckoned as mine; Ephraim and Manasseh will be mine, just as Reuben and Simeon are mine. Any children born to you after them will be yours; in the territory they inherit they will be reckoned under the names of their brothers (48:5–6).

This recognition would provide Joseph's boys with the same rights as the original set of Jacob's sons and their grandsons.

When Jacob saw the lads standing by, he asked for them to be brought closer so he could see them as he blessed them. Apparently his eyes were failing, as had his father Isaac's eyes, and he—of all people— did not want there to be an error in the giving of the paternal blessing! When they came close and Jacob could see the family resemblance, he embraced and kissed the boys with great affection (see 48:8–10).

Jacob said to Joseph, "I never expected to see your face again, and now God has allowed me to see your children too" (48:11). Jacob had mourned the loss of Joseph for much of his life and had relished the second chance he had been given to establish a relationship with him.

Joseph placed his sons to either side of Grandpa Jacob to receive his blessing—the one that should have been reserved for the eldest but that was being divided between the savior of the family and his sons.

> Joseph took both of them, Ephraim on his right toward Israel's left hand and Manasseh on his left toward Israel's right hand, and brought them close to him. But Israel reached out his right hand and put it on Ephraim's head, though he was the younger, and crossing his arms, he put his left hand on Manasseh's head, even though Manasseh was the firstborn (48:13–14).

Note that the old man crossed his arms, placing his right hand on Ephraim's head and his left on Manasseh's head. Then he said,

> May the God before whom my fathers Abraham and Isaac walked, the God who has been my shepherd all my life to this day, the Angel who has delivered me from all harm— may He bless these boys. May they be called by my name and the names of my fathers Abraham and Isaac, and may they increase greatly upon the earth (48:15–16).

When Joseph tried to switch his father's hands while explaining who was firstborn, Jacob refused, insisting, "I know, my son, I know. He too will become a people, and he too will become great. Nevertheless, his younger brother will be greater than he, and his descendants will become a group of nations" (48:19). Jacob continued as Joseph held his peace, knowing the blessing was inspired by God.

Jacob then addressed Joseph to say, "I am about to die, but God will be with you and take you back to the land of your fathers. And to you, as one who is over your brothers, I give the ridge of land I took from the Amorites with my sword and my bow" (48:21–22).

Jacob acknowledged what was already known by all—that Joseph had achieved a greatness far above his brothers. How fitting that Jacob gave a ridge above the plains as a special gift to Joseph—a place on high where everyone must lift their heads to see the one who completed God's prophecy.

Chapter 18

The Twelve Tribes of Israel

From Turbulent Waters to a Ravenous Wolf

Soon after his special blessing for Ephraim and Manasseh, Jacob assembled all his sons together to bid them farewell and bestow his knowledge of their future. Scripture makes no reference to Jacob's daughter, Dinah. Perhaps she was married and therefore someone else's responsibility. As Jacob blessed each son, some received kind words promising fame and prosperity, while others were reminded of their sins that would haunt them all their days. And like the destiny of humanity itself, a few would become notable, if not already, others would be hated, and some would be relegated to obscurity.

Jacob began with Reuben, the eldest:

> Reuben, you are my firstborn, my might, the first sign of my strength, excelling in honor, excelling in power. Turbulent as the waters, you will no longer excel, for you went up onto your father's bed, onto my couch and defiled it (49:3–4).

Reuben thought the episode with Bilhah had been forgotten. Wrong. Reuben had once been powerful and effective; he would be remembered as neither. Jacob continued,

> Simeon and Levi are brothers—their swords are weapons of violence. Let me not enter their council, let me not join their assembly, for they have killed men in their anger and

hamstrung oxen as they pleased. Cursed be their anger, so fierce, and their fury, so cruel! I will scatter them in Jacob and disperse them in Israel (49:5–7).

The legacies of Simeon and Levi would be just recompense for their treatment of others. Later, when the nation of Israel returned to Canaan after years of bondage in Egypt, Simeon's landholdings eventually would be absorbed into those allotted to Judah. Notably, the tribe of Levi would become the foundation of the priesthood. As those serving in the presence of God in the tabernacle and later in the Temple in Jerusalem, Levi's descendants would have plenty of time to atone for their violent past.

Judah was the first to receive anything that might be considered good news. Apparently his behavior had been noted during the recent days in Egypt:

> Judah, your brothers will praise you; your hand will be on the neck of your enemies; your father's sons will bow down to you. You are a lion's cub, O Judah; you return from the prey, my son. Like a lion he crouches and lies down, like a lioness—who dares to rouse him? The scepter will not depart from Judah, nor the ruler's staff from between his feet, until he comes to whom it belongs and the obedience of the nations is His. . . . He will wash His garments in wine, His robes in the blood of grapes. His eyes will be darker than wine, His teeth whiter than milk (49:8–12).

Judah's line would be the family to one day receive the Messiah—the One who would govern with power and authority. The prophecy also gives an image of the sacrifice of Christ and a preview of Christ's return as conquering King with garments rolled in blood—not His own blood but those of His enemies, as Christ comes at the close of history to destroy sin and wrong.

Zebulun did not get much, but at least nothing negative was said. He "will live by the seashore and become a haven for ships; his border will extend toward Sidon" (49:13). Although the eventual area for this tribe would be landlocked, they would live near the Mediterranean Sea and modern–day Lebanon, close enough to benefit from maritime trade.

Jacob then called Issachar

> a rawboned donkey lying down between two saddlebags. When he sees how good is his resting place and how pleasant is his land, he will bend his shoulder to the burden and submit to forced labor (49:14–15).

Issachar's lot would not be easy despite having the resiliency of a tough little burro. (Or was he rawboned because he was tired, poorly fed, and mistreated?) What would appear to be a simple and comfortable start would one day be an oppressive existence. The tribe of Issachar would slide into a comfortable lifestyle of pagan practices and would lose the Lord's protection and favor. Gradually his lineage would be absorbed into Canaanite society, becoming servants and slaves.

Next came Dan's destiny, followed by the others: "Dan will provide justice for his people as one of the tribes of Israel." How true, since the famed judge Samson would be from the tribe of Dan—a tribe that would raise some of the most tenacious fighters in all of Israel's history. Jacob continues, however, down a darker path: "Dan will be a serpent by the roadside, a viper along the path, that bites the horse's heels so that its rider tumbles backward" (49:16–17). The tribe of Dan would have other notables in history, who would be famous for their cruelty and duplicity.

"Gad will be attacked by a band of raiders, but he will attack them at their heels" (49:19). He would be at war but hold his own. Gad would prove this to be true until the Assyrians and Babylonians defeated his tribe years later.

"Asher's food will be rich; he will provide delicacies fit for a king" (49:20), meaning that his portion of the inheritance would be fertile and prosperous. But such prosperity led to complacency and a lack of dependence on God.

"Naphtali is a doe set free that bears beautiful fawns" (49:21). He must have been the good looking kid in the family. Other than his looks, however, he is not commended for anything else.

Jacob then came to Joseph, offering a thankful benediction:

> Joseph is a fruitful vine, . . . whose branches climb over a wall. With bitterness archers attacked him; they shot at

him with hostility. But his bow remained steady, his strong arms stayed limber, because of the hand of the Mighty One of Jacob, because of the Shepherd, the Rock of Israel, because of your father's God, who helps you, because of the Almighty, who blesses you. . . . Your father's blessings are greater than the blessings of the ancient mountains, than the bounty of the age–old hills. Let all these rest on the head of Joseph, on the brow of the prince among his brothers (49:22–26).

Benjamin, the youngest—and the favored son until Jacob was reunited with Joseph—probably thought he had the best position. Thinking he would most certainly outlive the others and inherit the largest portion of the combined estate, he probably sat back, waiting patiently for his name to be called in turn. Readers of Scripture may have viewed Benjamin as an innocent up to this point, possibly because Joseph framed him in creating the deception that brought all the brothers back to Egypt. But was there another dynamic at work?

Jacob referred to his last son as "a ravenous wolf; in the morning he devours the prey, in the evening he divides the plunder" (49:27). Did Benjamin come to resent his brother Joseph and all he had accomplished in Egypt? Did Ephraim and Manasseh usurp the position that Benjamin felt was his? In any case, Benjamin had fallen away from the center of Dad's attention.

Benjamin's tribe would prove to be problematic at best. King Saul, Israel's first king, would be a "Benjamite." He would be tall and regal looking but prone to mental illness, disobedience, and sorcery. Later, the tribe of Benjamin would be nearly wiped out. Only the grace of God and a creative plan to kidnap wives would make it possible for the Benjamites to survive at all.

These twelve sons—some stable, some dysfunctional—formed the twelve tribes of Israel.

A Funeral, Forgiveness, and a Future

When Jacob finished giving his prophetic commentary, he called his sons close for some final words of instruction. "I am about to be gathered to my people. Bury me with my fathers in the cave in the field

. . . of Machpelah, near Mamre in Canaan," where his grandparents, parents, and wife Leah were interred (see 49:29–32). With his sons and their families accounted for and his words of prophecy spoken, Jacob "drew his feet up into the bed, breathed his last and was gathered to his people" (49:33). It was as if he was tucking himself in for a good night's sleep after a long day's toil.

Joseph was the most distraught over Jacob's death, and he "threw himself upon his father and wept over him and kissed him" (50:1). Joseph's time with Jacob had been of better quality, whereas the others had endured years of Jacob's nonsense and instability. They had taken the berating, the insults, and the heavy demands; and consequently, they related to their father on a completely different level. Maybe they missed him, or perhaps they breathed a sigh of relief knowing that his despotic control of their lives was finally over. And those sons who had just received the scathing comments about their character (or lack thereof) might have even felt a certain gladness that Jacob was gone as they started their search for the family silver.

Then Joseph ordered that his father be embalmed, and Scripture indicates that the mummification process took forty days to complete (see 50:2–3). The Egyptians, out of great respect for Joseph and all he had done, had a full seventy–day period of mourning—the length of time customarily reserved for high officials, not Hebrew shepherds. But they all knew that what made Joseph happy, made Pharaoh happy. And when Pharaoh was pleased, he was not waging war, increasing taxes, or making life difficult for the average citizen.

When the period of mourning was over, Joseph went to Pharaoh's court and asked to be allowed to bury Jacob in Canaan as requested. Pharaoh willingly agreed. All the members of Jacob's, Joseph's, and the brothers' households—servants as well as family—traveled to Canaan for the funeral. Accompanying them was a large contingent of Egyptian officials—all the dignitaries of Pharaoh's court and of Egypt! "A very large company," indeed! (see 50:4–9). I wonder if anyone bothered to locate Uncle Esau to let him know that his brother had died.

The funeral service, marked with loud wailing and weeping, lasted seven days. The Canaanites, observing that this was not just another family burial rite but something elevated to an entombment of a head–of–state official, commented, "The Egyptians are holding a solemn ceremony of mourning." That is why the place near the Jordan River where the lamenting occurred was named Abel Mizraim, meaning "mourning of the Egyptians" (see 50:10–11). After the burial, everyone returned to Egypt.

Once back, the brothers had a chance to talk about their future and their relationship with Joseph now that Jacob's death had severed that connection. "What if Joseph holds a grudge against us and pays us back for all the wrongs we did to him?" (50:15). Still feeling guilty for what they had done and still quick to manipulate the truth for their own benefit, they made up some final instructions of their own "on their father's behalf," hoping to temper any of Joseph's residual desire for retribution. They sent the message to Joseph in Jacob's words, which read: "I ask you to forgive your brothers the sins and the wrongs they committed in treating you so badly" (50:17). A simple "I was wrong" and "Please forgive me" might have settled the matter, and it would have been done honestly.

Nevertheless, when Joseph received the message, he was anything but vengeful. Instead, he wept. Did he weep for the brothers who still did not understand the plan of God that began with that first dream so long ago? Or did Joseph know the joy of realizing his full potential as the person God created him to be?

The brothers then came to Joseph and threw themselves at his feet, saying, "We are your slaves" (50:18). To the brothers' relief, Joseph calmly assured them of their safety as he had done before (see 45:5–8). He also knew that forgiving his brothers might teach them a far greater lesson than getting even ever would.

> Don't be afraid. Am I in the place of God? You intended to harm me, but God intended it for good to accomplish what is now being done, the saving of many lives (50:19–20).

The Apostle Paul echoes this sentiment when looking back on adversities he and others had faced, finally seeing "that in all things God works for the good of those who love Him, who have been called according to His purpose" (Romans 8:28). What happens to us is not always good, although the outcome can be if we allow the Lord to build our reliance on Him.

Not much is written about those last years in Egypt after forgiveness and kindness replaced years of sibling rivalry. The twelve tribes of Israel became prosperous with plenty of flocks and herds and little Hebrew children running all over the "land o' Goshen." (Maybe that is where that phrase came from.) Joseph lived in Egypt long enough to become a great–great–grandfather at 110 (see Genesis 50:22–23). Who would have thought things would have worked out so well? Only God.

Like his fathers before him, Joseph decided to make his funeral wishes known. It is interesting how people often seem to have a sense of their own mortality and impending death. Joseph called for his family and brothers' families and said, "I am about to die. But God will surely come to your aid and take you up out of this land to the land he promised on oath to Abraham, Isaac and Jacob" (50:24). Reminding them of the promise that God would come to their assistance, he asked them to bury him back in Canaan—not leave him in Egypt: "You must carry my bones up from this place" (see 50:25). This may not have been wise, however. How is it possible to insist on moving such a man of high stature in Egyptian society, especially when Egyptians thought they knew a thing or two about death and the hereafter?

Scripture does not indicate the amount of time between Joseph's request and his demise, but when he died, "they embalmed him, [and] he was placed in a coffin in Egypt" (50:26). Was it an elaborate sarcophagus or something more simple to reflect his Hebrew heritage?

Joseph had quite the adventure as God's Man of the Century—a life unequaled by any other member of his typically dysfunctional Genesis family. Finally—someone had understood what was required—and did it right.

The Genesis story ends with Joseph, but the pledge to bury him near his parents would not be fulfilled until the Exodus: "And Joseph's bones, which the Israelites had brought up from Egypt, were buried at Shechem in the tract of land that Jacob bought" (Joshua 24:32). Joseph finally does return home, but as a lifeless mummy. We can come home, too, through a restored relationship with God made possible by Jesus and the new covenant of grace. But as for the rest of the Joseph saga that might be best titled "The Mummy Returns," that is a story for another time.

Epilogue

Are We Doomed to Repeat the Past?

The death of Joseph closes the account of the Genesis family, but it is, by no means, the end of the story. Moses, author of both the Book of Genesis and Book of Exodus, recaps the family composition as he begins his next narrative by listing all of Jacob's sons—the nucleus of the nation Israel. Eventually "Joseph and all his brothers and all that generation died, but the Israelites were fruitful and multiplied greatly and became exceedingly numerous, so that the land was filled with them" (see Exodus 1:1–7).

They must have been fruitful indeed because they grew from a total of seventy people (when everyone moved to Egypt at Joseph's request) to over 600,000 at the time of the Exodus 430 years later (see Exodus 12:37). A later reference, citing contributions to the construction of the Tabernacle based on population, states the number of those "twenty years old or more" was 603,550 (38:26). Some estimates have placed the Hebrew population during the Exodus into the multiple millions if the women, children, and those born along the way were included in the census.

Regardless of the exact count, the number of Hebrews increased to the extent that native Egyptians might have felt like a minority in their own country. Sadly, the Egyptians discovered the best way to take back control was to use the Hebrews as slaves to do their most dangerous and disagreeable tasks.

To the Hebrews' consternation, a new king replaced the Pharaoh of Joseph's day—one with no frame of reference concerning pledges of security and protection made by the prior administration. The Hebrew population was seen as a threat to national security if not turned into a ready–made labor force. They were put to work building the treasure cities of Pithom and Rameses, making their "lives bitter with hard labor in brick and mortar and with all kinds of work in the fields; in all their hard labor the Egyptians used them ruthlessly" (Exodus 1:14).

The Hebrews continued to multiply despite this abusive treatment, as they dreamed of their return to Canaan and their inheritance. To achieve that end, the Lord specially guarded one who would grow up in Pharaoh's household to learn the ways of the Egyptians. He would be the one to receive the law of God and be Israel's deliverer—Moses. But the story of the Exodus is more than Moses' *deliverance* of the Jews from bondage. It emphasizes their *inheritance* from the Lord that was begun in Genesis.

Inheritance is such an important concept that the word is used 215 times throughout Scripture, and what makes the concept significant is that we inherit from *family*—not from associates or associations. Furthermore, the future of our being, our immortality, will not exist—spiritually, theologically, or eternally—through relationships of like–minded colleagues, but as a family of kindred hearts.

Inheritance and Tradition

In Chuck Swindoll's book, *The Strong Family*, the author states that parents have to help build a child's sense of him– or herself in four aspects: identity, responsibility, authority, and conformity. Children need to have these components well established early in life if they hope to mature into healthy adults with emotional and spiritual vitality. I agree with Swindoll and would also add two more defining aspects—a sense of inheritance and a sense of tradition. These two concepts are closely related, almost interchangeable, yet the first is understood in terms of what is received, by privilege or by right; the second is grounded by what is learned, and practiced, and ultimately given back.

Along with the china, silverware, and genetic characteristics, we inherit patterns of thought and behavior that become our traditions—

a perpetual legacy in itself. The Genesis family demonstrated that, and as is the case for some families, hurts of the past are perpetuated from generation to generation, sometimes remaining unspoken, unforgiven, and unresolved.

Sometimes, too, we inherit things that have little or no value except for the pleasant memories they evoke. When my grandfather died, I inherited his "potato rock," which had been acquired on a past family outing. We had stopped for a picnic lunch beside a mountain stream, and as we were getting ready to leave we discovered Grandpa (a good Irishman to the end) out on a boulder midstream, fishing out a rock that looked like a perfect spud. It is just a worthless stone except to those who know the story that created a precious memory.

After Moses had brought the Hebrews out of Egypt and Joshua led them across the Jordan River into Canaan, ending the meandering migration that took over forty years, Joshua instructed a representative from each of the tribes of Israel (all of Jacob's sons) to take a rock from the middle of the river. "In the future, when your children ask you, 'What do these stones mean?' tell them . . . these stones are to be a memorial to the people of Israel forever" (see Joshua 4:4–7). These future generations would be reminded of how God had secured them safely across the river and through hard times. Our personal "stones of remembrance" help us recall those significant occasions and special people whose lives we have inherited through memory, as we form our own traditions of thanks.

God's Family

During the darkest days of World War II, Winston Churchill was asked what was needed to win the war, and he replied with eloquent succinctness, "Never give up. Never, never, never give up." We should heed this advice every day: Never give up—on each other, on God, or on His plan for us. The Lord never gave up on the first dysfunctional family in Genesis. Why? Because they were more than an association; they were family—and so are we.

Is that why the Lord kept restating the covenant—to make sure the Genesis family would not give up and would remember that He promised a homeland for Jacob's sons and his descendants?

God still cheers on His family: "I believe in you. We can do this together, because I love you and have adopted you into My family because My love never quits." He promises us a new relationship through Christ, where frail humankind can find grace to be healthy in body, mind, and spirit. God promises us the means to live in a vibrant family relationship with Him and with our brothers—our adopted siblings, in which no one is loved more than another. He loves us all, in exactly the way we need.

The Lord has made similar pledges of inheritance to all who trust in Jesus for the forgiveness of sin by giving His Spirit as a deposit, guaranteeing the completion of the promise. "For no matter how many promises God has made, they are 'Yes' in Christ. . . . He anointed us, set his seal of ownership on us, and put his Spirit in our hearts as a deposit, guaranteeing what is to come" (2 Corinthians 1:20–22).

From the lessons of Adam and Eve and the sons of Abraham, the generations of Genesis—have we learned to appreciate what we have inherited and what we have been promised from God? Do we only recognize its value after age or illness, calamity or our own stupidity takes it from us? Like the Pharaohs of Egypt, do we enslave ourselves by repeating the sins we have been taught? Do we still ignore the warnings? Do we leave behind stones of remembrance?

How Did God Teach His Family?

The Hebrew language indicates God as being "other" and unlike anything that was, is, or ever will be—He is distinct from what He has created. Therefore, He needed to create that same sense of "otherness" in His people without in any way ignoring their sinfulness because that would compromise His holiness and perfection. He wanted to make them "a chosen people, a royal priesthood, a holy nation, a people belonging to God, that you may declare the praises of Him who called you out of darkness into His wonderful light" (1 Peter 2:9).

But the Lord first had to reveal to His people how to behave so that the dysfunctional Genesis family and their heirs could know the character of God and how to survive in relationship to His holy presence. God needed, as Dr. John Oswalt of Asbury Seminary says, "to teach dry grass how to live in the blast furnace of God's holiness."

How did God show them the way? They certainly had not obeyed in the Garden of Eden when things were perfect. They had not learned from Cain and Abel, for they still killed each other. They had not learned from Abraham and Isaac because they still lied, or learned from Isaac and Rebekah since they still favored one child above another.

His people did not learn from the Flood and the destruction of Sodom and Gomorrah and continued to rebel, knowing they would incur the devastating wrath of God. They did not even learn from Joseph, for they still abused and enslaved their brothers.

In the Garden of Eden, God had given few instructions other than "don't mess with the forbidden trees." The extended Genesis family would require more defined parameters—a set of laws—so they could learn to live within established boundaries. Establishing boundaries, however, was and is never easy because humanity has always resembled a kind of spiritual chameleon. We like to blend into our surroundings. Was that not the fate of Issachar's tribe? And Lot's family, living near the perverse influence of Sodom, became just like them. Throughout the Bible, in fact, whenever the people of God lived in close proximity to evil, they *became* evil rather than witnessing for good. But the Lord kept His Word—and never gave up.

So after the Hebrews' liberation from slavery, God did something different. He extended the privilege of living in a covenant relationship to everyone rather than a select few individuals like Adam, Noah, and Abraham. The Lord set forth the terms of this new covenant, based on law, in the tenth chapter of Deuteronomy. Moses states

> What does the Lord your God ask of you but to fear the Lord your God, to walk in all His ways, to love Him, to serve the Lord your God with all your heart and with all your soul, and to observe the Lord's commands and decrees (Deuteronomy 10:12–13).

But the covenant was conditional. If the people obeyed, then the Lord would provide, protect, and cherish. If they did not, then He would be as unyielding in judgment as He is tender in His forgiveness.

> I am setting before you today a blessing and a curse—the blessing if you obey the commands of the Lord your God

> . . . the curse if you disobey . . . and turn from the way
> that I command you today (Deuteronomy 11:26–28).

If you trust, if you obey, if you believe—then you will receive, you will inherit the blessings of the family of God.

The account of the covenant service states that Moses had several young bulls sacrificed and cut into pieces. According to John Oswalt, Moses and God passed symbolically through the spaces between the pieces of the slaughtered animals to ratify the terms of the agreement, as if Moses had been warning God's people: "May what happened to these bulls also happen to you if you break this pledge." But the people violated the agreement just weeks later with the Golden Calf incident (see Exodus 32).

It was our ancestors who broke the pledge, though, not God. The Lord's program failed not because His plan was flawed but because the human heart was completely corrupted. If God had operated strictly from His justice, then we would have ended up like the bulls. Instead, the Lord made a new covenant—one engraved on our hearts, our lives, our character.

We are called to be like God, as closely as a child can resemble a parent. Like Adam, we were created in His image, but we needed to be recreated in His righteous character. And the only way that could have happened was for the Lord to change our hearts. Because of humanity's inherent predisposition toward wrong, something else was required:

> I will make a new covenant. . . . It will not be like the
> covenant I made with their forefathers when I took them
> by the hand to lead them out of Egypt, because they did
> not remain faithful to my covenant. . . . This is the
> covenant I will make. . . . I will put My laws in their
> minds and write them on their hearts. I will be their God,
> and they will be My people. . . . I will forgive their
> wickedness and will remember their sins no more
> (Hebrews 8:8–12).

With God's new covenant, He created a restored sense of family and belonging—just the way it was intended from the beginning. And He made the change from the inside.

The Hall of Faith

In the New Testament, the Book of Hebrews explains how the dysfunctional Genesis family, and we by extension, came to know the Lord in a deeper, more personal way. In Genesis we see the dysfunctional family in "real time." The Book of Hebrews shows several members of the family after they have been inducted into the "Hall of Faith," for it is by faith alone that they became functional.

The Bible defines faith as "being sure of what we hope for and certain of what we do not see. This is what the ancients were commended for" (Hebrews 11:1–2). Many times our reading ends there, and we are satisfied without knowing the application of what that faith accomplished to change the direction of humankind. If we continue to read, we see more.

The process of faith begins with the realization that God created it in the first place:

> By faith we understand that the universe was formed at
> God's command, so that what is seen was not made out of
> what was visible (11:3).

This oblique reference is to Adam and Eve. They were not there to see Creation happen, but they were the first to have it explained by the Creator Himself. Adam and Eve were not named in Hebrews because of their failure to believe God's threats, as well as His blessings, thus allowing sin into the world to spoil God's perfect plan.

Abel saw the principle of sacrifice with the eyes of faith:

> By faith Abel offered God a better sacrifice than Cain did.
> By faith he was commended as a righteous man, when
> God spoke well of his offerings. And by faith he still
> speaks, even though he is dead (11:4).

He trusted the Lord, knowing that the heart of the person offering the sacrifice was far more significant than the sacrifice itself. Abel believed the Lord wanted a sacrifice of joy, freely given. With an attitude like that, he could have offered bean sprouts and the Lord would have been pleased.

Of all the Genesis family members, Enoch was the only one who had relationship and faith in perfect harmony:

> By faith Enoch was taken from this life, so that he did not experience death; he could not be found, because God had taken him away. For before he was taken, he was commended as one who pleased God. And without faith it is impossible to please God, because anyone who comes to Him must believe that He exists and that He rewards those who earnestly seek Him (11:5–6).

Not only did Enoch please God and know Him, he earnestly sought after Him and eagerly accepted the rewards of unbroken fellowship.

Noah didn't have to see the deluge to be convinced—he trusted the Lord for what was coming long before things started getting wet:

> By faith Noah, when warned about things not yet seen, in holy fear built an ark to save his family. By his faith he condemned the world and became heir of the righteousness that comes by faith (11:7).

Abraham received the greatest coverage in Hebrews chapter eleven since he is father of many nations, founder of three of the world's great religions, and ancestor of humanity, fulfilling an improbable promise:

> By faith Abraham, when called to go to a place he would later receive as his inheritance, obeyed and went, even though he did not know where he was going. By faith he made his home in the promised land like a stranger in a foreign country; he lived in tents, as did Isaac and Jacob, who were heirs with him of the same promise. For he was looking forward to the city with foundations, whose architect and builder is God.
>
> By faith Abraham, even though he was past age—and Sarah herself was barren—was enabled to become a father because he considered Him faithful who had made the promise. And so from this one man . . . came descendants as numerous as the stars in the sky and as countless as the sand on the seashore (11:8–12).

Not one of these people had verifiable data to support the hope that the Lord's promises would be kept. All they had was God's word, and that was enough. Some never lived to see the end result of their trust (see 11:13). Since each had only a small segment of the covenant, they knew the promises of God would likely come to pass long after they were gone. Abraham could not have imagined the countless millions, including Jesus, who have known him as one of their ancestors.

Then the Book of Hebrews records the day that Abraham faced the greatest challenge of his life—the day he offered Isaac as a sacrifice:

> By faith Abraham, when God tested him, offered Isaac as
> a sacrifice. He who had received the promises was about
> to sacrifice his one and only son, even though God had
> said to him, "It is through Isaac that your offspring will
> be reckoned." Abraham reasoned that God could raise the
> dead, and figuratively speaking, he did receive Isaac back
> from death (11:17–19).

Abraham knew that everything he had of value was a gift from God, including Isaac. Having that kind of faith keeps one from becoming too attached to anything or anyone other than God.

Isaac only gets one brief mention, no doubt because of his dysfunctional behavior: "By faith Isaac blessed Jacob and Esau in regard to their future" (11:20). Faith was all that kept Isaac from being remembered as just a deluded old man.

Jacob does not fare much better for all his misadventures: "By faith Jacob, when he was dying, blessed each of Joseph's sons, and worshiped as he leaned on the top of his staff" (11:21). Jacob's blessing to Ephraim and Manasseh was truly inspired by God and delivered with clarity and insight. Sometimes what is done at the end of one's life is worth all the nonsense that precedes it.

The last member of the original Genesis family to make the roll was Joseph, who did not want to have his bodily remains stay in Egypt. He had faith that the Lord wanted to provide a home—and Joseph wanted to go there, even if the journey was made after his death:

> By faith Joseph, when his end was near, spoke about the
> exodus of the Israelites from Egypt and gave instructions
> about his bones (11:22).

All of these servants of God, in their own way, understood faith as the key attribute that propelled them from being flawed and miserable to being useful and productive. Faith was the one thing that freed their potential.

And like these patriarchs, faith grants each new generation—all of us—the opportunity to be free from slavery to sin. For us, the atoning, substitutional death and resurrection of Jesus Christ paid the price and penalty for sin to make us clean so God could recreate His holy nature and character in His people. We do not have to lie, steal, kill, or cheat—because the Lord is not like that. He has a different standard.

Unlike the old covenant, our relationship with Him is a matter of "want to" rather than "have to," a matter of love rather than obligation. And because of the new covenant of grace, our predisposition toward dysfunction can end. Those who were broken can be well adjusted, well balanced, resilient, obedient, and complete.

God's love is everlasting, unconditional—and in excess of anything we deserve. He is not surprised by anything we do or think since He has seen it all—from Adam to you and me—and loves us anyway. What a wonder!

CREST BOOKS

The Salvation Army National Publications

CREST BOOKS was established in 1997 so contemporary Salvationist voices could be captured and bound in enduring form for future generations—to serve as witnesses to the continuing force and mission of the Army.

Living Portraits Speaking Still: A Collection of Bible Studies

Leadership on the Axis of Change

Sanctified Sanity: The Life and Teaching of Samuel Logan Brengle

A Word in Season: A Collection of Short Stories

Andy Miller: A Legend and a Legacy

Pen of Flame: The Life and Poetry of Catherine Baird

If Two Shall Agree:
The Story of Paul A. Rader and Kay F. Rader of The Salvation Army

Fractured Parables:
And Other Tales to Lighten the Heart and Quicken the Spirit

Our God Comes: And Will Not Be Silent

A Salvationist Treasury:
365 Devotional Meditations from the Classics to the Contemporary

Slightly Off Center! Growth Principles to Thaw Frozen Paradigms

He Who Laughed First: Delighting in a Holy God

Easter Through the Years: A War Cry Treasury

Who Are These Salvationists? An Analysis for the 21st Century

Romance & Dynamite: Essays on Science & the Nature of Faith

A Little Greatness

Pictures from the Word

Celebrate the Feasts of the Lord:
The Christian Heritage of the Sacred Jewish Festivals

Christmas Through the Years: A War Cry Treasury

Never the Same Again:
Encouragement for New and Not-So-New Christians

Crest Books publications can be purchased through your nearest
Salvation Army Supplies and Purchasing department:

ATLANTA, GA—(800) 786–7372
DES PLAINES, IL—(847) 294–2012
RANCHO PALOS VERDES, CA—(800) 937–8896
WEST NYACK, NY—(888) 488–4882